World War II, Film, and History

WORLD WAR II,
FILM, AND HISTORY

EDITED BY

John Whiteclay Chambers II

David Culbert

New York   Oxford

OXFORD UNIVERSITY PRESS

1996

Oxford University Press

Oxford   New York
Athens   Auckland   Bangkok   Bogotá   Bombay
Buenos Aires   Calcutta   Cape Town   Dar es Salaam
Delhi   Florence   Hong Kong   Istanbul   Karachi
Kuala Lampur   Madras   Madrid   Melbourne
Mexico City   Nairobi   Paris   Singapore
Taipei   Tokyo   Toronto

and associated companies in
Berlin   Ibadan

Published by Oxford University Press, Inc.
198 Madison Avenue, New York, New York 10016

Oxford in a registered trademark of Oxford University Press

Library of Congress Cataloging-in-Publication Data

World War II, film, and history / edited by
John Whiteclay Chambers II. David Culbert.
p. cm.
Includes bibliographical references and index.
ISBN 0-19-509966-4.
ISBN 0-19-509967-2 (pbk.)
1. World War, 1939–1945—Motion pictures and the war.
I. Chambers, John Whiteclay II. II. Culbert, David.
D743.23.W67   1996
791.43'658—dc20   95-49890

9 8 7 6 5 4 3 2 1

Printed in the United States of America
on acid-free paper

To the Fellows and Staff

The Rutgers Center for Historical Analysis 1993–1995 Project "War, Peace, and Society in Historical Perspective"

Preface

Controversies during the fiftieth anniversary of the ending of World War II—the mishandled nature of the commemoration at Auschwitz, the exclusion of the Germans from D-Day observances, the arguments over the Smithsonian Institution's proposed exhibit on the *Enola Gay,* and the American use of the atomic bomb—demonstrate that half a century later the memory of World War II remains bitterly contested.[1]

Since this was the deadliest war in the history of the world, with more than 60 million persons killed,[2] continued bitterness is hardly surprising. What is particularly significant, however, is how different countries—indeed, sometimes different groups within countries—have separate memories and divergent ideas about how and what should be commemorated. As German President Roman Herzog suggested in 1995: "If you want to unify this Europe of ours, you have to bring its histories into line. You can't have a situation where national histories continue to persist, and each country picks out the good things it did."[3] Or, as William Faulkner noted, speaking of the states of the former Confederacy, "The past is not dead. It's not even past." While the sound of gunfire may end with the war, the battle can continue long afterward. In a story about contested remembrances of World War II, the *New York Times* noted in 1995 that "public memories of the past are also the battlefields of the present."[4]

As the generation that experienced the war diminishes in number, the public memory of it is increasingly shaped by those who create or manipulate the images of that conflict. For many people who lived through the war and even more for those who came later, their remembrance or understanding of World War II is contained most powerfully in visual images. Many of these images have became virtually universal: Hitler and massed ranks of Nazi flags; goose-stepping, steel-helmeted, leather-booted German soldiers; a jut-jawed, strutting Mussolini; Japanese soldiers attacking under the banner of the rising sun; Stuka dive bombers; great-coated Russian soldiers charging across the snow; British "Tommies" in shorts in the African desert; Patton with his ivory-handled pistols; the ubiquitous American jeep; Marines raising the American flag on Iwo Jima; the piles of corpses and skeletal survivors at the Nazi concentration camps; and the terminating symbols of the war—the atomic bomb's mushroom cloud and the Japanese surrender ceremony on the deck of the battleship USS *Missouri*.

World War II was probably the most photographed war in history. It began in Asia in 1937, in Europe in 1939, and did not end until 1945. During those years, military and civilian photographers and camera operators produced millions of pictures of the wartime experience, covering both the home front and the battle front in countries around the globe.

This book concerns the role of filmic historical interpretation in regard to World War II, from the images of combat with which people entered the war, to wartime use of film histories to mobilize nations, to the ways in which film and video have subsequently been used to portray and interpret that global conflict. It is a book about war, film, and history—and the continually evolving dynamic between the past and the present, moving images and their meaning, history and its representation. Audiences for moving images, particularly "blockbuster" television miniseries such as *Holocaust* (U.S., 1978) and *The Winds of War* (U.S., 1983), are so great that in recent times more people are experiencing the war through feature films and television docudramas than actually participated in it.

With modern telecommunications, the power of moving images has never been greater, nor their audience larger. Addressing the need for critical viewing of motion picture and video representations of the past, this book explores the relationship of history and film through several lenses—reflecting the perspectives of different countries, groups, and times—to suggest the ways in which visual images shape our understanding of World War II.

New Brunswick, N.J.   J.W.C.
Baton Rouge, La.   D.C.
February 1996

NOTES

1. Jane Perlez, "Confusion Marks Polish Plan to Commemorate Auschwitz," *New York Times,* January 16, 1995, p. A2; James E. Young, ed., *The Art of Memory: Holocaust Memorials in History* (New York: Prestel, 1994); Craig R. Whitney, "D-Day + 50 Years: Still Battling for Omaha Beach," *New York Times,* March 20, 1994, p. A8; Peter Schneider, "Invasions and Evasions" [Op-Ed], *New York Times,* June 7, 1994, p. A23; Craig R. Whitney, "Onlookers at D-Day Rites, Germans Are Ambivalent," *New York Times,* June 9, 1994, p. A8. See also "V-E Day Plus 50: Mixed Memories," *New York Times,* May 9, 1995, pp. A1, A10, A11. On the controversy over the *Enola Gay* exhibit at the Smithsonian Institution, see S. Budiansky, "A Museum in Crisis," *U.S. News & World Report,* February 13, 1995, pp. 73–75; Charles Krauthammer, "History Hijacked," *Time,* February 13, 1995, p. 90; Kai Bird, "Silencing History," *Nation* February 20, 1995, pp. 224–25; and "History and the Public: What Can We Handle? A Round Table About History After the *Enola Gay* Controversy," *Journal of American History* 82, no. 3 (December 1995): 1029–1144.

2. The casualty figure is from Gerhard Weinberg, *A World at Arms: A Global History of World War II* (New York: Cambridge University Press, 1994), p. 894.

3. Roman Herzog, quoted in Christian Habbe and Donald Koblitz, "Dresden's Undying Embers," *New York Times,* February 12, 1995, p. E15.

4. Gustav Niebuhr, "Whose Memory Lives When the Last Survivor Dies," *New York Times,* January 29, 1995, p. E5.

Contents

Foreword

ERIK BARNOUW

The twentieth century, a century of films, has also been a century of wars. From the start, filmmakers were beguiled by military matters, as is suggested by early film portrayals, such as *German Dragoons Leaping the Hurdles* (1896) and *The Charge of the Austrian Lancers* (1896), prominent in early programs of Auguste-Marie and Louis-Jean Lumière, French film pioneers. In retrospect, it can be seen that in shooting such training maneuvers, film people were themselves in training, getting ready for more powerful things to come.

The Lumière brothers wanted to catch life *sur le vif*—"live"—and they and their well-trained *opérateurs* did so with remarkable success, at home and abroad, in short films like *Workers Leaving a Factory* (1895), *Arrival of a Train* (1895), *Feeding the Baby* (1895), *Arrival of the Toreadors* (1896), *A Gondola Scene in Venice* (1896), and *Melbourne Races* (1896)—all living capsules of middle-class life. But military events were erupting, near and far. Filmmakers had more trouble coping with these. The action flared in inconvenient places. England's James Williamson therefore shot *Attack on a Chinese Mission Station* (1898), about an episode in the nationalist Boxer Rebellion, in his backyard; the Edison Company shot *Capture of a Boer Battery by the British* (1900), about the Boer War in South Africa, somewhere in West Orange, New Jersey; and a snowy Long Island meadow served as the setting for the Biograph Company's *Battle of the Yalu* (1904), about the Russo-Japanese War. Such moving pictures were sometimes called reconstructions. They served the cause of not only economy but also journalistic speed. Exhibitors were impatient for product; audiences were learning to be likewise.

Some cameramen did hurry to Cuba in 1898 for images of the Spanish-American War, but found a different problem. On film, the "charge up San Juan hill" by Theodore Roosevelt and his "Rough Riders" looked like a slow walk, hardly conveying a destiny-charged hour. The American naval victory at Santiago also proved difficult to capture. Two young film magicians, Albert E. Smith and J. Stuart Blackton, provided what was needed. Their *Battle of Santiago Bay* (1898) was shot in Blackton's kitchen on an upside-down table lined with waterproof canvas, holding an inch of water. Cutouts of Spanish and U.S. naval vessels, bought from a street vendor, were mounted on cardboard and placed in the water. Each was attached on its back to a strip of wood to make it stand. On each piece of wood was a pinch of gunpowder. Thin wires were used to explode these in rapid succession, amid thick clouds of cigar smoke provided by Mrs. Blackton, who suffered coughing spasms but stuck to her post. Blackton set off the explosions and agitated the water. The scene was a triumph in theaters. Film magic of this sort would come to be known as special effects.

Every new war seemed to add to filmmaking problems. Mexico's revolution and civil war, erupting in 1910, brought fame to Francisco "Pancho" Villa—a bandit to some, a Robin Hood to others. His daring cavalry raids kept the Mexican army on the run. He was elusive. His deeds were chronicled in newspapers. Why not in movie theaters? The Mutual Film Company finally caught up with him and got him to sign a contract (it is now located in the Library of Congress). Villa would cooperate; an up-front payment of $25,000 sealed the deal, which was a bargain for the company. (Did it occur to Mutual that it was helping to finance civil war?) For the sake of the cameramen, Villa agreed to fight his battles as much as possible during daylight. If an action went on beyond dusk, he agreed to do a reenactment at some convenient time. Finally, Mutual agreed to provide uniforms—presumably to counter the bandit image of Villa's forces. Filmmakers must have had some sense that their "actualities" were turning into fiction and that the distinction between the two was eroding.

In spite of such halting beginnings of filmmaking of wars and other historic events, a book published in Paris in 1898, *Une nouvelle source de l'histoire,* had already claimed for film a crucial historiographic role. It was written by one of the Lumière Company's agents, Boleslas Matuszewski, a Pole, who said that films—like coins, stamps, ornamental pottery, and sculpture—should be preserved in museums or special archives as "slices of public and national life." These images would be far more meaningful to the young, said Matuszewski, than the words in books. The depository should contain, he argued, not only moving pictures of meetings of rulers and departures of troops and squadrons, but also "the changing face of the cities." He recognized that history does not always happen where one awaits it, and that results are easier to find and photograph than causes. He predicted that the camera would often want to penetrate where it was not wanted, but that, in so doing, it could shed valuable rays of light. Film evidence, he said, would be able to shut the mouth of the liar. He saw motion pictures playing an important role in many fields, including that of war and the military.

Despite the problems and fumblings of the early years, many people would say that these predictions have come true. War-related films have created many interpretive problems, but even so the record is impressive. A number of war films are counted among the classics of the medium. Many viewers credit war films with providing special moments of revelation or inspiration.

How was all this success possible? Have producers changed their ways? Have they given up reenactments? By no means: Reenactments remain a tool of documentary and fiction producer alike, used in many war films. Have they given up magic trickery? By no means: Special effects have become an industry in themselves, brilliantly used in various classics. In truth, there is scientific wizardry behind every moment of every broadcast or film. Would you call a presidential broadcast a fake because you learned that technically you had not really seen the president, but had actually watched a reconstitution in beads of light of portions of a magnetic recording of words spoken some hours earlier, presumably by him? The range of illusion is great. Producers deceive the viewer at their own peril. Yet the complex technologies of our media do open the doors to skullduggery. The need for recognizing media deception becomes ever more pressing.

This book is an important contribution to media literacy, to the ability to "read" and understand the visual media. Here a number of words-on-paper historians, whose art has centuries of tradition behind it—during which its practices have been endlessly examined and weighed—survey the works of a newer kind of historical interpreter, whose specialities are images and sounds—in this case, the images and sounds of the filmic portrayal of war.

World War II, Film, and History

Introduction

JOHN WHITECLAY CHAMBERS II

DAVID CULBERT

"War is cinema and cinema is war," French critic Paul Virilio asserts, and he is not far from the mark.[1] Film and television depictions of war have evolved into the perceived "reality" of war.

War films—including antiwar films—have established the prevailing public images of war in the twentieth century. For American audiences, the dominant image of trench warfare in World War I has been provided by features such as *All Quiet on the Western Front* (U.S., 1930) and *Paths of Glory* (U.S., 1957). The image of combat in World War II remains shaped for American audiences by films like *Sands of Iwo Jima* (U.S., 1949) and *The Longest Day* (U.S., 1962), which portrays D-Day. Despite claims for the impact of widespread television coverage of the Vietnam War, it is probably pictures like *Apocalypse Now* (U.S., 1979) and *Platoon* (U.S., 1986) that have provided a subsequent generation with the most powerful images of what is seen as the "reality" of that much disputed conflict.

The perception of the "reality" of warfare through derivative assembled moving images began, as Erik Barnouw reminds us in his foreword, during the earliest years of motion pictures. The action and drama that war offered proved irresistable. By projecting movement and heightened emotion, motion pictures could go far beyond still photographs in capturing the "reality" of war and more palpably evoking the accompanying sense of danger, horror, and excitement.

During World War I, silent news footage was shot—or partly restaged—in war zones. After the war, vivid dramatic feature films shaped public

3

perceptions of the nature of fighting on the western front. Over the following decade, Hollywood produced several epics: *The Four Horsemen of the Apocalypse* (U.S., 1921), *The Big Parade* (U.S., 1925), *What Price Glory* (U.S., 1926), and *Wings* (U.S., 1927). In 1930, the powerful antiwar film *All Quiet on the Western Front* used a combination of pictures and sound to project an image of waste and hopelessness in modern, industrialized warfare in the West. A decade later, much of that grim image was overcome, or at least displaced, by a new faith in mechanized and mobile warfare, to convince a subsequent generation to fight in another world war.

World War II was a cinematic war. From the outset, governments and national motion-picture industries used moving images—newsreels, documentaries, and feature films—to help mobilize populations for war.[2] The armed forces of every major nation employed photographers who used lightweight 16–mm cameras to capture many aspects of the war (and stage or reenact some others[3]) to provide usable images for military and civilian purposes.

Motion pictures provided an effective means of building unity in World War II in part because audiences in urban, industrialized nations, such as the United States, had become accustomed in the preceding decades to going to movie theaters regularly as a way of obtaining information and entertainment. By the 1940s, more than half of the potential American audience went to the movies at least once a week.[4] In the interwar period, particularly with the adoption of sound film technology in the late 1920s, Hollywood refined its ability to produce films that delivered a message while they entertained.

In World War II, the cinematic experience was shared by civilians and combatants alike, as the mainly black-and-white films (and a few in color) made during the conflict were seen by those at home as well as members of the armed forces abroad. The experience crossed social and economic lines. Indeed, the leaders of most of the major nations were all film enthusiasts: Roosevelt, Churchill, Stalin, Mussolini, and Hitler had personal projectionists and private screening rooms for nightly viewing of dramatic and documentary films.[5]

After 1945, filmmakers—like novelists, historians, painters, and politicians—sought to represent and evaluate the war experience at home and at the front as well as to use that experience to provide a guide to the present. In the United States, the experience in a victorious war provided the basis for numerous features, including *A Walk in the Sun* (U.S., 1946),

Sands of Iwo Jima (U.S., 1949), *Twelve O'Clock High* (U.S., 1950), *Run Silent, Run Deep* (U.S., 1958), *The Longest Day* (U.S., 1962), *The Dirty Dozen* (U.S., 1967), *Patton* (U.S., 1970), *Catch-22* (U.S., 1970), *Tora! Tora! Tora!* (U.S. 1970), and *Midway* (U.S., 1976). They were some of the most popular that Hollywood has ever produced.

This book presents the insights of historians about selected historical films relating to World War II. Chronologically, these extend from *All Quiet on the Western Front,* the 1930 antiwar film that contributed to the pacifist and isolationist sentiment preceding World War II, to *Liberators* (U.S., 1992), the controversial documentary about the role of African-American troops in liberating Holocaust survivors from German concentration camps. The films discussed in this book were made in the United States, Japan, Germany, and the former Soviet Union.

The war film became a highly popular and powerful genre for generations of viewers.[6] Most movies are made in hopes of making a profit; some are artistic successes as well. A few such examples, from different countries, suggest the aesthetic richness of the genre: *All Quiet on the Western Front* (U.S., 1930), *Westfront, 1918* (Germany, 1930), *The Grand Illusion* (France, 1937), *Alexander Nevsky* (USSR, 1938), *In Which We Serve* (Britain, 1942), *The Best Years of Our Lives* (U.S., 1946), *Paths of Glory* (U.S., 1957), *Lawrence of Arabia* (Britain, 1962), *Battle of Algiers* (Italy–Algeria, 1965), *War and Peace* (USSR, 1966–1967), and *Apocalypse Now* (U.S., 1979).[7]

Moving images have played an important role in mobilizing the mass public for—or sometimes against—war. How they have done this and why—the relationship of filmmaking to politics and propaganda—is one of the topics explored in many of the chapters in this book. Another is the relationship between modern warfare and modern aesthetic experience—that is, to art and perception. For example, to what extent have images, derivative perspectives on the world, become the perceived sense of "reality" in contemporary culture? How much has this resulted from the cinematic representation of warfare in which people are separated from the real events and the mass horror of modern industrial warfare by layers of representational and interpretive distancing? How has the portrayal of particular images connected to war—which depict race, class, or gender, for example—reflected and contributed to larger cultural constructs? To what extent is war, at least the perception of it as represented by assembled moving images, a central part of modern consciousness?

The public memory of war in the twentieth century has been created less from a remembered past than from a manufactured past, one substantially shaped by images in documentaries, feature films, and television programs. A major part of that production has involved works depicting wars and battles long ended. Because they are so powerful in shaping our memory of the past, these historical films (ones that actively engage the discourse about historical events rather than simply use the past as an exotic background for a costume drama)[8] are of particular interest to students of history.[9] In addition, historians have begun to analyze various kinds of films and videos, especially in regard to the manner in which they reflect particular aspects of the society that created them and also, to the extent possible, the degree to which they influenced attitudes and behavior.[10] Questions about the aims, the accuracy, and the impact of visual depictions of earlier wars are addressed throughout this book.

The essays in this book derive from the conference "War, Film, and History," held October 21–23, 1993, at Rutgers University, New Brunswick, New Jersey, as part of a two-year study of "War, Peace, and Society in Historical Perspective" sponsored by the Rutgers Center for Historical Analysis.[11] Although the center generally focuses on written documentation and interpretation, the visual arts also provide essential historical perspective. The conference examined a number of films and television programs whose subject was prior wars, or, expressed differently, war as history.

Contributors also examine the relationship between moving images and the society and culture in which they were produced and received. Moreover, this book explores the use of film and video to inform and mediate perceptions about the nature of past wars. It also notes the importance of visual images in creating constructs of the so-called just and righteous war.

Every work of art reflects the society and culture in which it is created. Thus such works can serve as historical sources. To the degree that a particular film or video also influences people's attitudes and behavior, it can be seen as a historic force as well as a historical document.

Problems of representativeness and ambiguity make it difficult to use creative visual representations as cultural artifacts of the past, but such difficulties should not deter us. For art is one of society's most important methods for understanding itself, as Peter Paret reminds us in *Art as History: Episodes in the Culture and Politics of Nineteenth Century Germany*.[12] Indeed, works of art offer special insight into the nature of the past. If properly analyzed, artistic works, their creators, their background, and their impact can indicate connections among a number of components of society: aesthetic constructs, economic trends, political institutions, and sociocultural relationships.

Every film analyzed in this book tells us something about the cultural characteristics of groups in a specific historical time and place. That includes significant information about the perceived nature of war and peace and the self-identification of particular peoples and their adversaries. As antiwar films, such as *All Quiet on the Western Front,* demonstrate, motion pictures have sometimes been used to generate revulsion against warfare; but more often, film has portrayed war as idealistic, courageous, heroic, and glorious. It has also provided a powerful medium for mobilizing aggressive nationalistic feelings against other peoples—"the enemy"—and in this process, become an essential instrument of national policy.

A word about organization. The chapters in this book are arranged chronologically, in the order in which the visual documents were produced. Beginning with the United States in the interwar period, John Whiteclay Chambers II analyzes the classic antiwar motion picture, *All Quiet on the Western Front,* examining the film's production, assessing its reception in various countries, and noting the way in which images from this feature film have helped to define, even in our own era, the public memory of the "reality" of trench warfare on the western front.

In the Far East, the Japanese invasion and conquest of China that began in the late 1930s was portrayed to Japanese audiences in a variety of ways, each of which sought to legitimize Tokyo's aggressive imperialism. One technique is represented in *China Nights* (Japan, 1940). Freda Freiberg explains the mythic constructs in a genre of war films that seemingly took wartime romance and made it a metaphor for the Japanese conquest of China. In this first of a series of interracial melodramas, a manly and protective Japanese naval officer falls in love with a beautiful young Chinese street waif and molds her into a cultured, submissive wife. The melodramatic use of race and gender in a metaphoric justification of Japanese imperialism as driven by altruistic motives proved enormously popular with wartime Japanese audiences and provides important evidence about Japanese views of the war.

In Germany in the closing months of World War II, the Nazis released a lavish, historical feature film entitled *Kolberg* (Germany, 1945). Peter

Paret assesses the historical accuracy of *Kolberg* as a depiction of the siege of that German city by a French army in 1807, and he also explores the ways in which the film, released in January 1945, explicitly called for civilian sacrifice and last-ditch resistance. In an accompanying piece, David Culbert presents the newly published diary entries of Joseph Goebbels, the Nazi propaganda minister, to demonstrate how artistic considerations destroyed the timeliness of a film meant to mobilize German soldiers and civilians. Culbert contrasts *Kolberg* with *Das Leben geht weiter*, a feature still in production through mid-April 1945, also designed to instill in viewers the courage to live through daily Allied air raids.

In an examination of *Ivan's Childhood* (USSR, 1962) and *Come and See* (USSR, 1985), Denise J. Youngblood contrasts the way in which the "Great Patriotic War," as World War II is known in Soviet history, was made to serve the needs of the Soviet Union after Stalin's death. These films projected a patriotism informed as much by contemporary political concerns as by any guiding interest in historical accuracy.

Stephen E. Ambrose, analyzing *The Longest Day*, notes some of the problems involved in contrasting what we know about the historical reality of the Allied D-Day landings in Normandy on June 6, 1944, with the quasi-historical epic made by Darryl F. Zanuck in 1962. "Blockbuster" history, Ambrose believes, is better at giving viewers a sense of scale than accurately re-creating the way large-scale battles are actually fought. The major climactic moment in the film never even happened at Normandy.

Alice Kessler-Harris examines *The Life and Times of Rosie the Riveter* (U.S., 1980), a documentary about women defense workers on the American home front in World War II. While recognizing the selective use of evidence in the film, she emphasizes the degree to which the documentary's engaging main characters and its message of fair and equal treatment for female workers resonates with many contemporary viewers. The picture uses history to speak to the continuing dilemma in women's lives in modern America and to offer historical legitimacy to their drive for gender equity.

Clement Alexander Price contrasts *Men of Bronze* (U.S., 1980), the acclaimed documentary by William Miles about black American soldiers who fought in France in World War I, with *Liberators* (U.S., 1992), the controversial documentary by Miles and Nina Rosenblum that incorrectly claimed that African-American troops liberated Holocaust survivors at Dachau in April 1945. Whether driven by present-day social concerns or not, this film and its history offer a sobering reminder of the perils of film history based solely on a remembered past, rather than a fully documented history. In a separate chapter, originally written as a response to Clement Price's presentation, Daniel J. Leab, whose family had to flee Nazi Germany in 1938, discusses some of the problems of interpreting the Holocaust through the memory of black Americans.

The essays in this book offer case studies in some of the ways in which historians can approach films as historical documents. Historians ask quite specific questions about any picture being studied: Who made the film and why? Was there an unintended, as opposed to an intended, result? Did the filmmakers have a political agenda, either conscious or unconscious? Was the piece intended as propaganda? Who was the intended audience? To the extent possible to determine it, who was the actual audience? What does the history of the production suggest about conflicts at the time between political and artistic goals? What kind of reception did the work have—economically, aesthetically, politically? When analyzing films that take particular views of the past, it is important also to find out the nature of the historical debates in which these films are embedded. How do they contribute to the contested interpretations of the past?

This book also addresses several more general questions about the relationship of historians to filmmakers and film analysts. What is the most useful way to study film and video as an interpreter of history? In regard to war and film, why is there still a compartmentalization of inquiry in which military historians generally ignore feature films, and those who analyze war films rarely have a thorough grounding in the historiography of the period being portrayed. In general, then, what can be done to encourage interaction among historians and film scholars as well as filmmakers?

We see many benefits in the effort to bring historical analysis to bear on films that deal with the past, whether those visual works are fictional or documentary, whether docudrama or propaganda, whether instructional or escapist. We think, for example, that historical analysis of film's relation to war and to wartime society encourages a shrinking of the disciplinary boundaries separating fields, such as military history, diplomatic history, peace history, and film studies, and emphasizes a mutual interaction and benefit, including the integration of larger concepts, such as the connection between visual technology and national identity into a broader awareness of the richness of historical sources about World War II.

The unifying theme of *World War II, Film, and History* is that the visual representation of past wars is itself a cultural construction, reflecting social, political, economic, and cultural dynamics of the time. To an increasing degree, memory of wars won and lost, like other public memories, is a social construct. In this sense, World War II is increasingly a visual construct, a conflict remembered from the visual images now endlessly recycled in newspapers, in magazines, on television, and in motion pictures.

Providing a greater understanding of some of the visual images *in* that war and *of* that war—of the visual construction and interpretation of the past—is one of the primary aims of this book on World War II, film, and history.

NOTES

1. Paul Virilio, *War and Cinema: The Logistics of Perception,* 2d ed. (New York: Routledge, 1988), p. 26. For an equally insightful analysis, see Pierre Sorlin, "War and Cinema: Interpreting the Relationship," *Historical Journal of Film, Radio and Television* 14, no. 4 (Fall 1994): 357–66. Recent explorations of the relationship between war and film include "Guerra, cinema i societat" [War, Film and Society] [special issue], ed. J. M. Caparros-Lera, Sergi Alegre, and Luis Anyo, *Film Historia* 3, nos. 1, 2 (1993); and Karel Dibbets and Bert Hogenkamp, eds., *Film and the First World War* (Amsterdam: Amsterdam University Press, 1995).

2. On the use of visual images as a means of forging national unity in America in World War II, see Clayton R. Koppes and Gregory D. Black, *Hollywood Goes to War: How Politics, Profits and Propaganda Shaped World War II Movies* (New York: Free Press, 1987); Thomas Doherty, *Projections of War: Hollywood, American Culture, and World War II* (New York: Columbia University Press, 1993); Robert Fyne, *The Hollywood Propaganda of World War II* (Metuchen, N.J.: Scarecrow Press, 1994); and Roy Hoopes, *When the Stars Went to War: Hollywood and World War II* (New York: Random House, 1995). Censorship of images that were regarded as potentially disruptive of the war effort is examined in George H. Roeder, Jr., *The Censored War: American Visual Experience During World War Two* (New Haven: Yale University Press, 1993). For cinema and mobilization in other countries in World War II, see Anthony Aldgate and Jeffrey Richards, *Britain Can Take It: The British Cinema in the Second World War* (Oxford: Blackwell, 1986); Philip M. Taylor, ed., *Britain and the Cinema in the Second World War* (New York: St. Martin's Press, 1988); David Welch, *Propaganda and the German Cinema, 1933–1945* (New York: Oxford University Press, 1983); Hilmar Hoffmann, *"Und die Fahne führt uns in die Ewigkeit": Propaganda im NS-Film,* vol. 1 (Frankfurt: Fischer Taschenbuch, 1988); and Peter Kenez, "Black and White: The War on Film," in *Culture and Entertainment in Wartime Russia,* ed. Richard Stites (Bloomington: Indiana University Press, 1995), pp. 157–75.

3. For evidence of such visual material in World War II being staged or gathered from other sources, see Peter Maslowski, *Armed with Cameras: The American Military Photographers of World War II* (New York: Free Press, 1993); and James M. Skinner, *"December 7:* Filmic Myth Masquerading as Historical Fact," *Journal of Military History* 55, no. 4 (October 1991): 507–16.

4. Total weekly attendance by the "potential audience" (that is, everyone who had the ability to get to a motion-picture theater) soared in the United States from 31 percent in 1935 to 74 percent in 1945, according to Robert Sklar, *Movie-Made America: A Cultural History of American Movies,* rev. ed. (New York: Random House, 1994), pp. 269–71. For attendance figures in Europe, see Pierre Sorlin, *European Cinemas, European Societies, 1939–1990* (London: Routledge, 1991), pp. 81, 89, 152.

5. Martin Loiperdinger, Rudolf Herz, and Ulrich Pohlmann, *Führerbilder: Hitler, Mussolini, Roosevelt, Stalin in Fotographie und Film* (Munich: Piper Verlag, 1995).

6. A recent analysis of the war genre is in Jeanine Basinger, *The World War Two Combat Film: Anatomy of a Genre* (New York: Columbia University Press, 1986).

7. For extensive annotated lists of war films, see, for example, S. J. Curley and F. J. Wetta, *Celluloid Wars: A Guide to Film and the American Experience of War* (Westport, Conn.: Greenwood Press, 1992); Brock Garland, *War Movies: The Complete Viewers Guide* (New York: Facts on File, 1987); and Frederick A. Eiserman, *War on Film: Military History Education,* Historical Bibliography No. 6 (Fort Leavenworth, Kans.: U.S. Army Combat Studies Institute, 1987).

8. The distinction between mere costume dramas and historical films that engage the past is made eloquently by Robert A. Rosenstone, "Introduction," *American Historical Review* 97 (October 1992): 1138–41.

9. Pioneering works on the study of historical films (that is, films that portray, interpret, and engage the past) include Pierre Sorlin, *The Film in History: Restaging the Past* (Totowa, N.J.: Barnes & Noble Books, 1980); Barbara Abrash and Janet Sternburg, eds., *Historians and Filmmakers: Toward Collaboration* (New York: Institute for Research in History, 1983); Daniel J. Walkowitz, "Visual History: The Craft of the Historian-Filmmaker," *Public Historian* 7, no. 1 (Winter 1985): 53–64; "AHR Forum [on Portraying History on Film]," *American Historical Review* 93, no. 5 (December 1988): 1173–227; Anton Kaes, *From "Hitler" to "Heimat": The Return of History as Film* (Cambridge, Mass.: Harvard University Press, 1989); the essays in Bruce A. Murray and Christopher J. Wickham, eds., *The Historiography of German Cinema and Television* (Cardondale: Southern Illinois University Press, 1992); Leger Grindon, *Shadows on the Past: Studies in the Historical Fiction Film* (Philadelphia: Temple University Press, 1994); and Robert A. Rosenstone, ed., *Revisioning History: Film and the Construction of a New Past* (Princeton: Princeton University Press, 1995).

10. Use of audio-visual documents as sources of historical analyses has been encouraged by a number of individuals, organizations, and journals, such as *American Historical Review, Film & History, Film History, Historical Journal of Film, Radio and Television, Journal of American History, Journal of Contemporary History,* and *Vingtième siècle: revue d'histoire.* Among pioneering works are J. A. S. Grenville, *Film as History: The Nature of Film Evidence* (Birmingham: University of Birmingham Press, 1971); Paul Smith, ed., *The Historian and Film* (Cambridge: Cambridge University Press, 1976); John E. O'Connor, *Teaching History with Film and Television* (Washington,

12 **Introduction**

D.C.: American Historical Association, 1987); and Marc Ferro, *Cinema and History,* trans. Naomi Green (Detroit: Wayne State University Press, 1988). Important later collections include Steven Mintz and Randy Roberts, eds., *Hollywood's America: United States History Through Its Films* (St. James, N.Y.: Brandywine Press, 1993); Robert Sklar and Charles Musser, eds., *Resisting Images: Essays on Cinema and History* (Philadelphia: Temple University Press, 1990); John E. O'Connor and Martin A. Jackson, eds., *American History/American Film: Interpreting the Hollywood Image,* 2d ed. (New York: Continuum, 1988); Peter Rollins, ed., *Hollywood as Historian: American Film in a Cultural Context* (Lexington: University Press of Kentucky, 1983); K. R. M. Short, ed., *Feature Films as History* (Lexington: University Press of Kentucky, 1981); and "Historians and the Movies: The State of the Art" [special issues], *Journal of Contemporary History* 18, no. 3 (July 1983) and 19, no. 1 (January 1984). Appearing as this book went to press was "Cinema, the Time of History" [special issue], *Vingtième siècle: revue d'histoire* 46 (Spring 1995).

In addition, there is the study of the history of film, a somewhat different field dominated originally by students of film studies, but lately including professional historians as well. For example, see Garth Jowett, *Film: The Democratic Art: A Social History of American Film* (Boston: Little, Brown, 1976); Robert C. Allen and Douglas Gomery, *Film History: Theory and Practice* (New York: Knopf, 1985); the insightful piece by John Belton, "CinemaScope and Historical Methodology," *Cinema Journal* 28, no. 1 (Fall 1988): 22–44; Sorlin, *European Cinemas;* Miriam Hansen, *Babel and Babylon: Spectatorship in American Silent Film* (Cambridge, Mass.: Harvard University Press, 1991); Alan Williams, *Republic of Images: A History of French Filmmaking* (Cambridge, Mass.: Harvard University Press, 1992); Janet Staiger, *Interpreting Films: Studies in the Historical Reception of American Cinema* (Princeton: Princeton University Press, 1992); Douglas Gomery, *Shared Pleasures: A History of Movie Presentation in the United States* (Madison: University of Wisconsin Press, 1992); and Robert Sklar, *Movie-Made America: A Cultural History of American Movies,* rev. ed. (New York: Random House, 1994) and *Film: An International History of the Medium* (New York: Abrams, 1993).

11. A number of papers from that conference were published in "War, Film, and History" [special issue], *Historical Journal of Film, Radio and Television* 14, no. 4 (October 1994): 353–478.

12. Peter Paret, *Art as History: Episodes in the Culture and Politics of Nineteenth Century Germany* (Princeton: Princeton University Press, 1988).

1

All Quiet on the Western Front (U.S., 1930): The Antiwar Film and the Image of Modern War

JOHN WHITECLAY CHAMBERS II

More than any other American feature film in the interwar years, *All Quiet on the Western Front* (U.S., 1930) came to represent the image of World War I. In a poignant saga of the life and death of a sensitive young German recruit, the film vividly portrays the senseless horror of trench warfare on the western front. Explosive sound effects accompany powerful visual images—it was one of the first "talking" pictures—to produce an emotionally wrenching viewing experience. It directly contributed to the widespread revulsion against such slaughter and against industrialized mass warfare in general.

All Quiet on the Western Front became the classic antiwar movie, hailed as a brilliant and powerful work of film art and widely imitated.[1] It achieved that classic status for historical and political reasons as much as for the cinematographic excellence with which it brought to the screen the war novel of an embittered young German veteran and writer, Erich Maria Remarque.[2] For the film speaks to ideology and history as well as to art.

Half a century later, the very title remains highly evocative. It has emotional significance even for those whose understanding of World War I comes primarily from sepia pictures in history books. Now blended in public memory, the novel and film have come, like the young protagonist, the schoolboy-soldier Paul Bäumer, to symbolize the transformative horror of the western front. It is a horror that remains embedded in Western consciousness as a consequence of World War I.

The film was based on the tremendously popular novel *All Quiet on the Western Front* (in the original German, *Im Westen nichts Neues* [literally, Nothing New on the Western Front]). The book was a semiautobiographical work, based on Remarque's brief experience in the German army in the last years of the war. It was also clearly a product of the disillusionment that he and many other veterans felt about the war and about the dislocations of the postwar era.

Remarque wrote the manuscript in the winter of 1927/1928 when he was twenty-nine years old. Originally published in Germany in January 1929 and in Britain and United States six months later, the book sold more than 2 million copies within a year. (In the United States, the Book-of-the-Month Club made the work its June 1929 selection, and Little, Brown sold 300,000 copies the first year.) By the end of 1930, it had been translated into twelve languages and had sold 3.5 million hardbound copies worldwide. Fawcett Crest acquired the paperback rights in 1958, and the first 175,000 copies sold out in a few months. By the time Remarque died in 1970, this classic had been translated into forty-five languages and had sold nearly 8 million copies, a figure that by now has probably exceeded 12 million. The book sells well to the present day.[3]

After the publication of Remarque's semiautobiographical novel, there was considerable interest in his military record. He began his compulsory military service in November 1916, entering at eighteen with his school classmates. He underwent basic and advanced recruit training at the Caprivi Barracks in Osnabrück, his hometown in Westphalia. In June 1917, he was sent with the Second Guards Reserve Division to a position behind the Arras lines on the western front. Assigned to a sapper (engineer) unit, which had responsibility for laying barbed wire and building dugouts and gun emplacements, Private Remarque and his unit were subsequently transported to Flanders to help block the major offensive being prepared by the British and French.

On July 31, 1917, after two weeks of artillery bombardment, the Allies began their assault (called Third Ypres or Passchendaele by the British). On the first day, Remarque, who had been working in the sapper unit, was wounded in the neck, leg, and forearm by fragments from a British artillery shell. His wounds were serious enough for him to be taken to a hospital in Duisburg, Germany, where he underwent surgery and then spent more than a year in convalescence, working part-time as a clerk in the office helping to process the new casualties from the front. Released from the hospital on October 13, 1918, as fit for garrison duty, Remarque was transferred to a reserve unit in Osnabrück. He was declared fit for active duty on November 7, 1918, four days before the end of the war.[4] Although Remarque had spent only about six weeks at the front, his experience was reinforced by his time with wounded and dying soldiers at the hospital and by correspondence with his schoolboy comrades in his old unit, several of whom were later killed or severely wounded.

The 1930 Hollywood version of Remarque's book was the result of the successful judgment of Carl Laemmle, an independent entrepreneur who had entered the industry by purchasing theaters and then expanding into distribution and finally into production, heading the Universal Pictures Corporation. *All Quiet on the Western Front,* directed by Lewis Milestone, starred both a young, relatively unknown actor, Lew Ayres, and a seasoned veteran, Louis Wolheim.[5] Ayres became personally identified with the film, for he perfectly captured the role of the protagonist, the sensitive, educated, young man, Paul Bäumer—the everyman trapped, corrupted, and destroyed by the horror of trench warfare. Like the book, the 1930 film continues to be available, now on videocassette. In 1979, an entirely new version, in color, was produced for television, starring Richard Thomas and Ernest Borgnine.

In August 1929, Laemmle rushed from Hollywood to his native Germany and acquired the film rights from the author.[6] He put his twenty-one-year-old son, Carl Laemmle, Jr., the studio's new general manager, in charge of production of *All Quiet on the Western Front.*[7] The younger Laemmle ("Junior," as he was called) hired Lewis Milestone as the director.

Born in Russia, Milestone had abandoned an education in mechanical engineering in Germany in 1913 at the age of eighteen and gone to New York City to pursue a career in the theater. He soon became an assistant to a theatrical photographer. When the United States entered World War I in 1917, Milestone enlisted as a private in the photography section of the U.S. Army Signal Corps. In the army, he first worked on training films in New York, then learned about editing at the film laboratory of the War College in Washington, D.C., where he worked with Victor Fleming, Josef von Sternberg, and a number of future luminaries in the motion-picture industry. Discharged from the army in 1919, Milestone became a U.S. citizen and soon moved to Hollywood. He worked as an assistant film cutter, a screenwriter, and, beginning in 1925, a director.[8] In 1927, *Two Arabian Knights,* a tale of two fun-loving

American doughboys, earned Milestone the Motion Picture Academy Award for Best Comedy Direction.

Despite the objections of the younger Laemmle, Milestone hired Ayres, who was only twenty years old and largely unknown, for the starring role of Paul Bäumer.[9] Although inexperienced, Ayres had many of the qualities Milestone sought: he was handsome, earnest, intelligent, and somewhat broodingly introspective. Without a well-known actor in this leading role, the audience effectively saw the young soldier protagonist as a kind of everyman. Ayres's relative lack of experience was balanced by the veteran actor Wolheim, who personified Katczinsky (Kat), the knowledgeable, cynical, but compassionate oldtimer. It is Katczinsky who instructs the young recruits about how to try to survive in the deadly chaos of the front.

For the task of converting Remarque's novel into a screenplay for what the industry then referred to as a "talker," Milestone drew on a group of capable writers. Contrary to many accounts, playwright Maxwell Anderson was not responsible for the dramatic treatment; he simply wrote the first version of the dialogue.[10] Creating a chronological screenplay to replace the episodic form of the novel, Milestone and his associates helped give structure to a war-film genre: one that follows a group of young recruits from their entry into the military, through basic training, to the battlefront. In this case, the film begins with the young men together in the schoolroom just before they rush off to enlist, encouraged by their chauvinistic teacher, Kantorek, who shames them into enlisting and calls on them to become "Iron Men" of Germany.

The film, like the novel, emphasizes the war's senseless human waste, especially the waste of youth. The camera graphically illustrates the breakdown of romantic ideas of war, heroism, and defense of the nation in the squalor of the trenches and the brutality of combat. One by one, the young men are lost; finally death takes the veteran Katczinsky and shortly thereafter Paul himself. (Remarque ends his novel by stating that when Paul's body is turned over, "his face had an expression of calm, as though almost glad the end had come.")[11]

Milestone and his crew paid particular attention to the brutality and senselessness of war on the western front and to the sharp divergence between civilian and military society, between home front and battlefront. Civilian society is characterized by the strident chauvinism of influential males such as Paul's father and schoolteacher, or by the intense anguish of helpless women such as his mother and sister. In the training camp and at the front, civilian youths are transformed into soldiers. They form cohesive male fighting groups, bands of brothers. But the male bonding is not simply as a band of warriors but also, under the shock and pain of the war, as a family—caring, nurturing, even doing domestic chores—but a family without women.

The few women in this film have smaller roles. They, too, are victims. On home leave, Paul finds food in short supply, his mother ailing and out of touch with reality. At the military hospital, nurses and other medical personnel are overworked and unsympathetic. The book has little romantic interest, but Hollywood felt the need for some women and sex in the film. Indeed, one of the promotional posters used in the United States featured a pretty young French woman clearly alluring to the German schoolboy-soldiers as well as to potential ticket buyers. In a French village behind the German lines, three young women are so famished that they are willing to exchange sex for the soldiers' food rations. Although the book mentions this episode only briefly, Milestone expanded it into an important and moving sequence.

New motion-picture technology—sound equipment and more mobile cameras—gave "talkers" a distinct new feeling. Like many of the posters, paintings, and other art of the postwar period, film took on a new harder, sharper, more brutal aura. Milestone brought the brutal reality of the war to this picture. Together with his cinematographer, Arthur Edeson, the director used a combination of fast-moving sight and sound to heighten the impact of the violence of industrialized warfare. The two men built a number of powerful images: the pock-marked landscape of no man's land; flashes of artillery fire on the horizon; wisps of smoke and gas; soldiers climbing out of trenches and rushing into machine-gun fire and exploding artillery shells; bodies lying crumpled on the ground, hanging on barbed wire, or being hurled into the air by artillery blasts.

One of Milestone's most acclaimed—and imitated—photographic devices was a long, fast, parallel-tracking shot (moving sideways like a crab) along a German trench while maintaining its focus on the attacking French infantrymen. The shot was possible because Milestone mounted Edeson's camera on a giant wheeled crane so it could be rolled along behind the trench. In the film, for nearly a minute of uninterrupted camera movement, the picture travels rapidly along at eye level as machine-gun bullets mow down charging French *poilus*. When sound was added, the metallic staccato of the machine guns helped audiences believe they were *hearing* the authentic sounds of battle.

Milestone and Edeson drew on their experience in silent films to create appropriate visual imagery and movement. They shot the battle scenes with more maneuverable silent cameras, adding sound effects later. Outdoor dialogue scenes, however, were made with cameras and microphones. Edeson had been hired partly because he had developed a quieter camera whose whir would not be picked up by the microphone.

As cinematographer-historian George Mitchell has observed, Edeson used lighting and camera angles to particular effect.[12] He employed a low-key light level to emphasize the drama of the recruits' first nighttime barbed-wire duty and later to provide a claustrophobic effect of sustained artillery bombardment on the shell-shocked boys in their dugout. In one of the most important scenes—the shell-crater sequence—Edeson used a subtle but realistic lighting style to mark the passage from day to night to day again. At night, flashes of artillery fire light up the shell hole and its two occupants. With the morning light, a close-up reveals the dead French soldier's face, his eyes open and staring, as a wisp of smoke, a remnant from the battle, drifts into the frame. The camera cuts to Paul's anguished, pleading face. Thus the horror and remorse of individual killing is brought directly to the audience.

Universal worked to give an authentic World War I appearance to this historical drama, particularly since it was filmed in southern California, not northern France. Studio purchasing agents obtained actual French and German army uniforms as well as scores of tools, packs, helmets, rifles, machine guns, and even six complete artillery pieces. The focus on authenticity was in the visual details. As such, for example, the film illustrates the change in German army equipment during the war, from the initial spiked leather headgear (*Pickelhaube*) to the more practical steel helmets (*Stahlhelm*).

In the battle scenes, Milestone and Edeson produced some of the most effective pictures in the film. During the major attack sequence following the artillery bombardment, Edeson's main camera, mounted on a large crane, travels over the trenches as the German troops pour out of their dugouts and into position. It is joined by five other cameras shooting from different angles as French infantrymen charge toward the trenches and the mobile camera. Stern-faced German machine gunners open fire. The French are mowed down. Later in the editing room, Milestone repeatedly cut these shots with increasing brevity and speed. A hand grenade explodes in front of a charging *poilu*. When the smoke clears, all that remains is a pair of hands clutching the barbed wire. In the trench, Paul turns his face away in sickened revulsion. As the remaining French soldiers reach the trench, they lunge at the Germans with bayonets in hand-to-hand fighting. The Germans counterattack, but are temporarily halted by French machine guns. After taking the first line of French trenches, the German soldiers are ordered back to their own lines before the French can counterattack. The battle ends in a stalemate, each side exhausted and back in its original position.

Sound made action films such as *All Quiet on the Western Front* so powerful—the impact of music, the realism produced by the sound of rifle fire, the staccato rhythm of machine guns, and the deafening roar of exploding artillery shells. Milestone jolted his audience right onto the battlefield by simultaneously bombarding their senses and their emotions.

Milestone created powerful images of war for the public, but how did he, after having spent the war years in the United States, know the reality of combat? Milestone believed it had come from the year he spent in Washington, D.C., in the U.S. Army Signal Corps during World War I. There he had become quite familiar with photographic images of the war. As Milestone recalled in an interview published in 1969, "having examined thousands of feet of actual war footage while stationed at the Washington, D.C., War College during the war, I knew precisely what it was supposed to look like."[13] A decade later, he drew on that background in re-creating the battle scenes near Los Angeles. This is wonderfully suggestive phrasing by Milestone: what war was *supposed* to look like. He had never personally seen a battle or a battlefield. What he did was to draw on his experience with documentary photographic representation of the battlefront to create the "reality" for his dramatic representation of battle and the battlefront. He seems not to have questioned whether he was drawing on the illusions created by Signal Corps photographers, who were able to photograph battlefields only *after* the actual fighting.

The theme of disillusionment is heightened in *All Quiet on the Western Front.* The meaninglessness of the war is accentuated by having the front-line German soldiers discuss the fatuous nature of the official justifications from Berlin. However, it is most dramatically personalized in one of the key scenes of the film, the shell-crater scene. In the midst of battle, Paul, panic-stricken and hiding in a shell crater in the middle of no man's land, mortally stabs a French soldier who had leaped into the crater. While the Frenchman slowly dies, Paul begs his forgiveness, concluding that they are after all comrades forced to kill each other by the brutal mechanics of war. This certainly represents another powerful theme: all men are brothers.

The most unforgettable scene is the final one. On a quiet day shortly before the Armistice, Paul is killed by a French sniper's bullet as he reaches out to touch a butterfly just beyond the trench. Milestone juxtaposes the fragility and beauty of life against imminent death by means of ironic sound effects (a soldier's harmonica plays softly in the background) and by visual cross-cutting among shots of the French rifleman, Paul, and the butterfly. The camera focuses on a close-up of Paul's hand reaching out across the parched, lifeless earth to embrace life—the butterfly, which is also a symbol of Paul's lost innocence and youth, a reminder of his adolescent, butterfly-collecting days. But instead of life—death: the sharp crack of a rifle, the spasmodic jerk of Paul's hand, which slowly relaxes in death. The harmonica suddenly stops. The sensitive, young, schoolboy-soldier has become just another corpse in the trenches. It is, according to one observer, "one of the screen's most powerful, well-remembered moments."[14]

All Quiet on the Western Front was immediately hailed for its aesthetic excellence and trenchant realism. It officially premiered at New York City's Central Theater on April 29, 1930, a few days after opening at the Carthay Circle Theater in Los Angeles. Hearst's New York *American* reported that the film had played "before an audience stunned with the terrific power of stark, awful drama." The *New York Times* agreed that the spectators had been "silenced by its realistic scenes." "It is far and away the best motion picture that has been made . . . talking or silent," asserted the New York *Telegraph.*[15]

The film was a phenomenal financial success. "A money picture," reported *Variety,* the entertainment industry's weekly newspaper.[16] It actually cost $1.5 million to produce, a major sum for a motion picture at that time, and nearly double the $900,000 projected cost estimates. Universal was so embarrassed by the overrun that it publicized only $1.2 million.[17] Within two weeks after the premiere, however, it was evident that the studio would more than recoup its investment, even in the worst economic slump of the Great Depression. *All Quiet on the Western Front* broke box-office records and showed to sell-out crowds in city after city throughout the spring of 1930.[18]

Erich Maria Remarque first saw the film in August 1930. Universal's representative in London, James V. Bryson, flew to Germany with a print and provided a private showing for the author and his wife. Back in London the next day, Bryson told reporters that Remarque had said not a word during the showing but had "walked out of the theatre with tears in his eyes." According to Bryson, before parting Remarque had told him, "It is beautiful indeed. I can say no more."[19]

The success of *All Quiet on the Western Front,* the book and the film, convinced other studios to produce antiwar motion pictures. Two made in 1930 were particularly noteworthy both for their intrinsic merit and for their demonstration of the international nature of the phenomenon: *Journey's End* (Britain, 1930) and G. W. Pabst's *Westfront 1918* (Germany, 1930). Although James Whale's sound-film rendition of English veteran Robert C. Sherriff's play proved highly popular with British audiences and American critics, its lack of battle scenes limited its mass appeal in America. More comparable to Milestone was Pabst, whose artistry and "near documentary realism" were widely recognized and whose antiwar film based on the novel *Vier von der Infanterie* (Four Infantrymen) drew large audiences on the European Continent.[20]

From its first showing, *All Quiet on the Western Front* was recognized as a powerful emotional force for opposition to war, particularly modern industrialized mass warfare. Its message received support from many pacifists, liberals, and moderate socialists throughout Europe and, to some extent, in the United States as well.[21] But there was also considerable hostility to the film in many countries. Some cultural critics decried its horrifying images and its "vulgarities." Military and political opponents argued that it distorted and demeaned the patriotism and heroism of soldiers of all nations and that it undermined nationalism, military defense, and the ability to wage war. They considered it subversive pacifist propaganda.

German sensibilities had been evident in reactions to Remarque's book, which had been vehemently denounced by conservative nationalist opponents of the fledgling Weimar Republic. Consequently, the initial German-dubbed version prepared by Universal, finally released in December 1930, had included, with Remarque's consent, a number of cuts to obtain the approval of the Berlin Censorship Board. These cuts were not concerned with aspects controversial in other countries—others had objected to the use of earthy language and latrine scenes, the oblique bedroom scene of Paul and a young French woman, or the scene of Paul stabbing a French *poilu* to death—but with the image of Germany and the German army. Thus Universal, in the initial German version, deleted scenes showing the recruits beating up their tyrannical corporal, Himmelstoss, a symbol of Prussian militarism; soldiers starving for food and eating ravenously; soldiers blaming the kaiser and the generals for the war; the grim use of the boots of a dead comrade to show the loss of one soldier after another; and Paul's return to his former school and his antiwar remarks there.

Although *All Quiet on the Western Front* played to packed theaters in the United States, Britain, and a number of other countries, it was banned in Germany, first, for a time, by the Weimar Republic and then permanently in 1933 by the Nazi regime.[22] The German-dubbed film, which had opened to the general public in Berlin on December 5, 1930, almost immediately led to Nazi street demonstrations and theater disruptions.

Representatives of the German military and the War Ministry had already issued protests against the film for portraying German soldiers as ridiculous, brutal, and cowardly.[23] Now Nazi propaganda leader Joseph Goebbels took his brown-shirted toughs to the streets, directing a number of violent protests and demonstrations against what he characterized as "a Jewish film" filled with anti-German propaganda.[24] Inside the theaters, Nazis released snakes and mice and set off stink bombs.[25] Although both the Board of Censors and the government of Chancellor Heinrich Bruening denied that they were influenced by the Nazi demonstrations, the decision to ban the film was correctly seen as a capitulation to the right, including the Nazis. Pabst's antiwar film, *Westfront 1918,* produced in Germany, was being shown in many theaters without any disturbances or demonstrations. The Nazis had used the American film to force the issue, and they had won. Hailed in Germany by the nationalist press— Goebbels's newspaper called it "Our Victory"—the censorship decision was, nevertheless, denounced by most liberals and socialists there and throughout the West.[26]

The Bruening government's decision was vigorously attacked by the left-wing Social Democrats in Germany, but they were unable to lift the ban until late the following year. By June 1931, Universal Pictures was willing to make concessions to gain access to Germany, with 5,000 theaters the second-largest market in Europe. The Board of Censors lifted the general ban in September 1931 after Universal had agreed to eliminate the scene of Corporal Himmelstoss's cowardice at the front as well as Paul's panic in the graveyard attack, and Paul's contrition for having stabbed the French soldier to death. The shortened film (cut by nearly 900 meters, or approximately 33 minutes) played with great success in Germany through early 1932. Indeed, in 1931 and 1932, *All Quiet on the Western Front* was the sixth most popular film in Germany.[27]

Nazi-inspired censorship of the film had a lasting impact long after the debate in Germany in the 1930s. Indeed, it apparently had a long-term effect on the film and its showings in many countries. In its eagerness to enter the German market, Universal Pictures had agreed to delete offensive scenes not only from the film shown in Germany but from all versions released throughout the world.[28] Thus the versions of Milestone's *All Quiet on the Western Front* seen by millions of viewers in many countries for years thereafter were versions "sanitized" to please the German censors in 1931.

The history of the various versions and releases of *All Quiet on the Western Front* from 1930 to the present, as reconstructed in part by film scholar Andrew Kelly, demonstrates that Universal Pictures was as responsive to national sensibilities and political constraints as it was to economic opportunities in the international marketplace.[29] The film was banned entirely in Italy, Hungary, Bulgaria, and Yugoslavia. Austria, also under pressure from the Nazis, followed Germany's lead. The version shown in France (beginning in October 1930) did not contain the scenes of French women entertaining German soldiers and had a drastically cut shell-crater scene in which Paul kills the French soldier. Paris banned this and other antiwar films in 1938—the eve of World War II.[30]

In 1979, an entirely new, Technicolor version of *All Quiet on the Western Front* was shown on the CBS television network in the United States with subsequent release abroad in theaters and a decade later in videocassette.[31] The new version starred twenty-eight-year-old Richard Thomas as Paul and sixty-two-year-old Ernest Borgnine as "Kat" Katczinsky. It was financed by British film magnate Sir Lew Grade, who bought the rights from Remarque's widow, actress Paulette Goddard. Produced by Norman Rosemont, the remake was filmed somewhat paradoxically on the eastern front—in Czechoslovakia.

The nearly three-hour-long television format allowed the inclusion of a number of scenes from the book that had been omitted in the two-hour 1930 motion picture, such as a gas attack and a hospital sequence in which a blinded soldier tries to commit suicide by stabbing his chest with a fork. The 1979 film also captures and maintains the episodic intensity of the novel, keeping almost all the scenes brief and using a narrator, Paul Bäumer himself, to recount experiences and feelings, a role that Richard Thomas expresses with fine poetic shadings. Writer Paul Monash stuck much more closely than Milestone and his team to Remarque's original novel, employing flashbacks rather than straight chronology and, for example, softening a bit the character of Himmelstoss, who redeems himself in battle instead of remaining a sadistic and cowardly martinet.

Director Delbert Mann, whose career had led him to make television dramas from classic books, sought a harder edge and even more grue- some detail than the 1930 classic, drawing on standard techniques of late- twentieth-century American action movies: rapid cutting, extreme close- ups, as well as assault on the senses by intensified battle noise and excruciating specificity of blood and gore, including impacting bullets, retching gas victims, gaping wounds and flowing blood, rat-besieged corpses, and incinerating flame throwers—all in vivid color. In place of the "butterfly ending," the 1979 version created a new image directly dramatizing Remarque's cryptic conclusion where Paul had simply been hit and fallen face down. While most American reviewers heralded the 1979 remake as powerful and poignant, some in the United States and many in Europe, where it was shown in theaters in 1980, criticized the new film as uninspired. As one British reviewer put it, "This ploddingly expensive film is as redundant a remake as one could conceive."[32]

Milestone's version of *All Quiet on the Western Front* had enormous impact. Its ideological message contributed to political debate about war and isolationism in the 1930s and later. And in its most lasting impact, it helped to shape public images and attitudes about trench warfare, about World War I, and, to some extent, about modern war in general. It also had an undeniable impact on the motion-picture industry. It encouraged directors to shift away from static, stage-like "talking pictures" and instead to combine sound with open, fluid, visual movement. Milestone's long tracking shots were widely and specifically imitated. Of broader and deeper influence was his effective combination of sight and sound to produce a new realism that became one of the most influential concepts of Hollywood in the 1930s.[33]

No wonder, then, that pacifists, antiwar activists, and isolationists—in the 1930s and in subsequent decades—have regarded the film as a powerful antiwar and antimilitary device. Its many subsequent re- releases (in 1934, 1939, and 1950)[34] and the creation of an entirely new version in 1979 both reflected and contributed to such tides of sentiment in the United States and perhaps elsewhere. Indeed, Lew Ayres was so affected by his role and by the antiwar sentiment of the 1930s that he became a conscientious objector in World War II, at first refusing to be a soldier, and only after much public censure, agreeing to serve as an unarmed medic in the Army Medical Corps.

Most important, *All Quiet on the Western Front* helped shape subsequent public perceptions of the nature of trench warfare and of World War I. In part, this was because the book and the film, the latter with its visual images matching—even exceeding—the inner power of Remarque's writing, were part of the outpouring of antiwar memoirs and novels of the period that recast and bitterly articulated the failure of the Great War in the story not of battles won but of individual lives lost—and lost for naught.

Photography, especially motion-picture photography, is part of the explanation of why World War I has been so powerfully implanted on the public consciousness. It was the first war to be extensively recorded by motion-picture cameras, particularly by official military and newsreel photographers of all the major belligerents.[35]

Because of inherent dangers in no man's land, the weight and immobility of the early cameras, and official restrictions of access to the front, actual infantry combat was seldom recorded on film. However, some enterprising cameramen staged simulated battle scenes using soldiers and trenches near the front. Audiences were unaware of this deception, and as with *The Battle of the Somme,* a full-length British documentary shown in London theaters in the autumn of 1916 within weeks of the onset of the battle, viewers thought they were seeing actual combat footage.[36] Such motion-picture images, together with the many black-and-white still photographs, created an entire audience who thought they had a real view of the war, despite the fact that they had not seen combat firsthand.

Widespread accessibility of photographic images gave World War I a mass audience, but it was an audience whose understanding of the "reality" of war was in fact mediated through images, just as much as it was interpreted by the printed word. Our visual image of World War I has for generations been informed by the grainy, black-and-white pictures of the western front. The original photographs were dictated in part by the bulky nature of the cameras and the limitations of their lenses, and in part by the restrictions placed on the photographers by the military authorities who rigorously controlled access to the front.

The dramatic films of World War I, whether the silents of the war years and the 1920s or the sound films of the 1930s, beginning with *All Quiet on the Western Front,* drew directly on those original images to build a sense of realism. Consequently, our image of the war is still dominated by the "reality" authenticated by such film footage. Indeed, one of the most jarring aspects of watching the 1979 television version of *All Quiet on the Western Front* was precisely its vivid color and smooth, modern film style, a format that so clearly separates it from the now distant war it portrays.

The popularity of *All Quiet on the Western Front* and some other antiwar films may also be due in part to more oblique reasons. Despite their so-called realism and their brutal images, the antiwar films of the 1930s about World War I may, as historian Jay M. Winter has suggested, actually have helped masses of people take the chaos and horror of the war and mentally organize them in a more understandable and manageable way. Most of these motion pictures, after all, focus on the surface of events, on action, on melodrama, usually even including some romance, or at least on a bit of comedy. In mythologizing the war (re-creating the conflict in a form more understandable and acceptable than the complex and chaotic event itself), such films offer a way to organize and contextualize events that are themselves fragmented and traumatic. They serve to "help people to bury the past and help people recreate it in a form they can accept," according to Winter.[37] In more generic terms and in a longer time frame, antiwar action pictures, from *All Quiet on the Western Front* to the anti–Vietnam War film *Apocalypse Now,* offer many viewers both the moral solace of a strong, antiwar message and the emotional appeal of an exciting, action-filled adventure.[38]

Regardless of how World War I is understood, it is clear that in cinematographic terms, the enduring public perceptions of the image of trench warfare were established in the 1930s. No single motion picture was more influential in fixing that visual representation than this one. After *All Quiet on the Western Front,* the "reality" of trench warfare in the public mind was a "reality" constructed in Hollywood.

NOTES

1. See, for example, Martin Gilbert, *The First World War: A Complete History* (New York: Holt, 1994), p. 535; and Michael T. Isenberg, *War on Film: The American Cinema and World War I, 1914–1941* (London: Associated University Presses, 1981), pp. 30, 132, 138. Historical studies of the film's place in the larger political and cultural history of the period have been few and largely fragmentary—for example, Andrew Kelly, "*All Quiet on the Western Front:* Brutal Cutting, Stupid Censors and Bigoted Politicos, 1930–1984," *Historical Journal of Film, Radio and Television* 9, no. 2 (1989): 135–50;

Jerold Simmons, "Film and International Politics: The Banning of *All Quiet on the Western Front* in Germany and Austria, 1930–1931," *Historian* 52, no. 1 (November 1989): 40–60; and Richard A. Firda, *"All Quiet on the Western Front": Literary Analysis and Cultural Context* (New York: Twayne, 1993), pp. 92–106. In a class by itself is Modris Eksteins, *Rites of Spring: The Great War and the Birth of the Modern Age* (London: Black Swan, 1990), pp. 368–97. A useful anthology is Bärbel Schrader, ed., *Der Fall Remarque: Im Westen nichts Neues: Eine Dokumentation* (Leipzig: Reclam-Verlag, 1992). An earlier, if longer, version of this chapter appeared as John Whiteclay Chambers II, " 'All Quiet on the Western Front' (1930): The Antiwar Film and the Image of the First World War," *Historical Journal of Film, Radio and Television* 14, no. 4 (October 1994): 377–411.

2. On his early life, see Christine R. Baker and R. W. Last, *Erich Maria Remarque* (London: Oswald Wolff, 1979), pp. 5–17.

3. Erich Maria Remarque, *Im Westen nichts Neues* (Berlin: Ullstein Verlag, 1929); Remarque, *All Quiet on the Western Front*, trans. A. W. Wheen (Boston: Little, Brown, 1929). A recent translation is Remarque, *All Quiet on the Western Front*, trans. Brian Murdoch (London: Jonathan Cape, 1994). In this chapter, all citations are to Wheen's translation, which is more widely read.

Remarque died in 1970, and two major collections of materials related to him and his work have now become available: the Erich Maria Remarque Papers at the Fales Library, New York University, New York (cited hereafter as Remarque Papers), and the Erich Maria Remarque Archive/Research Center on War and Literature at the University of Osnabrück in Germany. I am indebted to Tilman Westphalen, Thomas F. Schneider, Claudia Glunz, Dieter Voigt, Michael Fisher, Annegret Tietzeck, and Nicole Figur for their assistance in my research in Osnabrück.

4. See the detailed investigation by Remarque's friend and biographer Hanns-Gerd Rabe, "Remarque und Osnabrück," *Osnabrücker Mitteilungen* 77 (1970): 211–13. The fullest account in English is Harley U. Taylor, Jr., *Erich Maria Remarque: A Literary and Film Biography* (New York: Lang, 1989), pp. 15–21.

5. *All Quiet on the Western Front* (Universal Pictures, 1930). Original sound version is 138 or 140 minutes, black-and-white (a silent version with synchronized music and sound effects ran longer). Carl Laemmle, Jr., producer; Lewis Milestone, director; George Abbott, Maxwell Anderson, and Del Andrews, screenplay; C. Gardner Sullivan, story editor; Arthur Edeson, director of photography; George Cukor, dialogue director; and David Broekman, music. The cast included Lewis Ayres (Paul Bäumer), Louis Wolheim (Katczinsky), George "Slim" Summerville (Tjaden), John Wray (Himmelstoss), Raymond Griffith (Gerard Duval), Russell Gleason (Müller), Ben Alexander (Kemmerick), Arnold Lacy (Kantorek), and Beryl Mercer (Mrs. Bäumer); in the silent version, Zasu Pitts (Mrs. Bäumer); Marion Clayton (Miss Bäumer); and Yola D'Avril (Suzanne).

6. "Confers on New War Film," *New York Times*, August 11, 1929, p. A8.

7. "Mr. Laemmle Returns [from Germany]. Universal's President Discusses Film *All Quiet on the Western Front*," *New York Times*, October 6, 1929, sec. 9, p. 8.

8. Lewis Milestone and Donald Chase, "Milestones" (typescript of unfinished autobiography in the Lewis Milestone Collection, Margaret Herrick Library, Academy of Motion Picture Arts and Sciences, Los Angeles [cited hereafter as Milestone Papers]; Joseph R. Millichap, *Lewis Milestone* (Boston: Twayne, 1981).

9. See the somewhat differing accounts of Ayres's selection in the interview with Lewis Milestone, in Charles Higham and Joel Greenberg, *The Celluloid Muse: Hollywood Directors Speak* (Chicago: Regnery, 1969), pp. 152–54; and William Bakewell, *Hollywood Be Thy Name* (Metuchen, N.J.: Scarecrow Press, 1991), pp. 71–72.

10. See, for example, Millichap, *Milestone*, p. 39. Maxwell Anderson acknowledged a less important role (Anderson, interview, May 10, 1956, Columbia University Oral History Collection, New York).

11. Remarque, *All Quiet on the Western Front,* p. 291.

12. George J. Mitchell, "Making *All Quiet on the Western Front*," *American Cinematographer* 66 (September 1985): 34–43.

13. Milestone, interview in Higham and Greenberg, *Celluloid Muse,* p. 151. He told this story many times.

14. Mitchell, "Making *All Quiet on the Western Front*," p. 42. Milestone tried several different endings during production. See mimeographed copies of the shooting script, November 20, 1929, Remarque Papers, Series 1, Folder 4; and the continuity script, undated, Film Studies Center, Museum of Modern Art, New York City.

15. Excerpts in an advertisement by Universal Pictures, *Variety,* May 7, 1930, pp. 36–37.

16. [No first name given] Sime, Review of *All Quiet on the Western Front, Variety,* May 7, 1930, p. 21.

17. For the $1.2 million publicized figure, see ibid. The projected estimate was $891,000, according to "Estimated Cost Sheets," December 9, 12, 1929; the actual cost was $1,448,863.44, "Final Cost Sheet," May 7, 1930 (*All Quiet on the Western Front* file, Universal Pictures Collection, Doheny Library, University of Southern California, Los Angeles).

18. "Disappointments on [West] Coast Last Wk [*sic*]—'Western Front' Made Big Showing, $22,000 at $1.50 Top," *Variety,* April 30, 1930, p. 9; "Only 'Western Front' at Over Capacity, $21,957, in $2 Central," *Variety,* May 14, 1930, p. 8.

19. "Bryson Meets Remarque. 'All Quiet' Author Moved to Tears," *Bioscope,* August 6, 1930; James V. Bryson, "I Meet Erich Remarque," *Cinema,* August 6, 1930 (clippings in Scrapbook, vol. 3, Milestone Papers). I am indebted to Sam Gill, archivist, Margaret Merrick Library, Academy of Motion Picture Arts and Sciences, for calling my attention to these articles.

20. On Whale's film based on the R. C. Sherriff play, see D. J. Wenden, "Images of War 1930 and 1988 *All Quiet on the Western Front* and *Journey's End:* Preliminary Notes for a Comparative Study," *Film Historia* 3, nos. 1–2 (1993): 33–37. On Pabst's film, see Michael Geisler, "The Battleground for Modernity: *Westfront 1918* (1930)," in *The Films of G. W. Pabst,* ed. Erich Rentschler (New Brunswick, N.J.: Rutgers University Press, 1990), pp. 91–102.

21. Modris Eksteins, "*All Quiet on the Western Front* and the Fate of a War," *Journal of Contemporary History* 15, no. 2 (April 1980): 355.

22. Simmons, "Film and International Politics"; Heiko Hartlief, "Filmzensur in der Weimarer Republik. Zum Verbot des Remarque-Films *Im Westen nichts Neues*: Eine Fallstudie im Geschichtsunterricht der gymnasialen Oberstrufe," *Erich Maria Remarque Jahrbuch* 3 (1993): 73–82.

23. U.S. Ambassador, Germany, to Secretary of State, December 17, 1930, received January 3, 1931, in *Foreign Relations of the United States, 1931* (Washington, D.C.: Department of State, 1931) vol. 2, pp. 309–10. (Hereafter cited as *FRUS*)

24. Diary entries, December 5–12, 1930, Joseph Goebbels, *Die Tagebücher von Joseph Goebbels: Samtiche Fragemente*, ed. Elke Fröhlich (Munich: Saur, 1987), vol. 1, pp. 641–45.

25. "Fascist Youth Riot as *All Quiet* Runs," *New York Times*, December 9, 1930, p. 17.

26. "Unser der Sieg! [Our Victory!]," *Der Angriff*, December 15, 1930, p. 1; Guido Enderis, " 'All Quiet' Banned by Reich Censors," *New York Times*, December 12, 1930, p. 12; *New York Times*, [editorial], "Commercialism and Censorship," December 13, 1930, p. 20.

27. Simmons, "Film and International Politics," pp. 58–59; U.S. Ambassador, Germany, to Secretary of State, September 12, 1931, in *FRUS*, pp. 316–17; see also "Top 10 Films in Germany, 1925–1932" [table], in Joseph Garncarz, "Hollywood in Germany: The Role of American Films in Germany," in *Hollywood in Europe: Experiences of a Cultural Hegemony*, ed. David W. Ellwood and Rob Kroes (Amsterdam: VU University Press, 1994), pp. 123–24.

28. U.S. Ambassador, Germany, to Secretary of State, September 12, 1931, *FRUS*, p. 316.

29. Andrew Kelly, "*All Quiet on the Western Front:* 'Brutal Cutting, Stupid Censors, and Bigoted Politicos, 1930–1984," *Historical Journal of Film, Radio and Television* 9, no. 2 (1989): 135–50.

30. Although some studies claim that the film was not shown in France until 1963, a silent version with French intertitles (and perhaps some simulated sound effects) opened there in October 1930. In December 1930, the German-dubbed sound version with French sub-titles brought the full impact of the battle scenes as well as the dialogue to enthusiastic French audiences. Apparently it was not until 1950 that a French-dubbed dialogue sound version was released. See "*A l'Ouest, rien de nouveau vient d'être présenté à Marseille*," *La Cinématographie française*, no. 624, October 17, 1930, p. 197; Fernard Morel, "Le Cinéma doit préparer la paix; on doit détaxer les films de ce genre," *La Cinématographie française*, no. 625, October 25, 1930, p. 49; "La Foire aux films," *L'Humanité*, November 23, 1930, p. 4; Emile Vuillermoz, "Le Cinéma: 'A l'Ouest, rien de nouveau,' " *Le Temps*, December 27, 1930, p. 5; and, for the re-release, Henry Magnan, "Le Cinéma: 'A L'Ouest rien de nouveau' Durable chief-d'oeuvre," *Le Monde*, December 30, 1950, p. 8.

31. *All Quiet on the Western Front* (Sir Lew Grade's Marble Arch Productions, England, 1979), three hours, premiered on CBS, November 14, 1979. Delbert Mann, director. The cast included Richard Thomas, already known for playing John Boy in the TV series *The Waltons* (Paul Bäumer); Ernest Borgnine (Katczinsky); Ian Holm (Himmelstoss); Donald Pleasence (Kantorek); and Patricia Neal (Mrs. Bäumer). A videocassette, running 131 minutes, was released by ITC, Avid Home Entertainment, in 1992.

32. John Pym, review in the British *Monthly Film Bulletin*, quoted in James Robert Parish, *The Great Combat Pictures: Twentieth Century Warfare on the Screen* (Metuchen, N.J.: Scarecrow Press, 1990), p. 16.

33. Millichap, *Milestone,* pp. 24–25; see also Michael I. Isenberg, "An Ambiguous Pacifism: A Retrospective on World War I Films, 1930–1938," *Journal of Popular Film and Television* 4, no. 2 (1975): 98–115.

34. Copies of the scripts for the 1930, 1934, and 1939 releases are in the New York Film Censor Records, New York State Archives, Albany, New York. I am indebted to Richard Andress, archivist, for providing these.

35. On photographing the western front, see Paddy Griffith, *Forward into Battle* (Chichester: Bird, 1981), pp. 43–74; Geoffrey Malins, *How I Filmed the War* (London: Jenkins, 1920); and S. D. Badsey, "Battle of the Somme: British War Propaganda," *Historical Journal of Film, Radio and Television* 3, no. 2 (1983): 99–115.

36. Roger Smither, " 'A Wonderful Idea of the Fighting': The Question of Fakes in *The Battle of the Somme,*" *Historical Journal of Film, Radio and Television* 13, no. 2 (1993): 149–68.

37. Jay M. Winter, *The Experience of World War I* (New York: Oxford University Press, 1989), p. 328.

38. Milestone himself went on to direct a number of war and antiwar films, among them *The General Died at Dawn* (1936), *The Purple Heart* (1944), *A Walk in the Sun* (1946), *Halls of Montezuma* (1951), and *Pork Chop Hill* (1959).

2

China Nights (Japan, 1940): The Sustaining Romance of Japan at War

FREDA FREIBERG

Japan's war against China, lasting as it did continually from 1937 to 1945[1] and engaging the bulk of the Japanese Imperial Army, was fundamental to Tokyo's goals in Asia. This chapter examines Japanese wartime cinema, most particularly the motion picture *China Nights* (Japan, 1940), and analyzes some of the ways in which the war in China was represented on film to wartime Japanese audiences. It also demonstrates the effectiveness of using gender analysis to comprehend the ways in which the war was portrayed as an interracial and sexual melodrama. In the militaristic Japanese projection, feminine China needed the subjugation and protection of virile, masculine Japan. As analysis of the film makes clear, racism and sexism were important components of Japanese imperialism in China.

A number of Japanese motion pictures from the 1930s and 1940s have survived,[2] and the film industry of wartime Japan has received considerable attention from scholars and other students of Japanese culture. In their studies of propaganda in Japanese movies, neither the American researchers in wartime Washington[3] nor the postwar historians of Japanese film[4] made a sharp distinction between pictures made before and after the attack on Pearl Harbor (December 7, 1941), when Japan entered World War II against the United States and the Western Allies. Scholars largely examined works made before Pearl Harbor, films focusing on the Japanese conquest of China. They generally found the Japanese war movies more subtle in their propaganda—far less jingoistic and melodramatic than their American counterparts. Yet historical accounts of the Japanese film industry have identified a steady increase in government control over the industry from the early 1930s to the early 1940s.

The military campaigns and conquests in Asia and the Pacific in the 1930s and early 1940s gave an impetus to the Japanese film industry by opening new markets for the distribution of its products in the occupied territories, offering exotic new locations for film production, and providing opportunities for extensive experience in newsreel and documentary production at the battlefronts and in the occupied territories. Personnel were sent to the occupied areas for the purposes of producing, distributing, and exhibiting the films that would serve Japanese cultural and military interests. In short, they would establish and run film companies.

Japanese filmmakers who were pacifists, antimilitarists, or simply critical of the government's policies did not flee to countries at war with their homeland. Rather, they tended to go into self-imposed "exile" in the occupied territories, supervising the production of films by conquered peoples in Manchuria, China, or Indonesia, for example. Some of them fully intended to foster the culture and film skills of the indigenous people, but ultimately they remained tools of Japanese imperialism, subject to the policies of the military forces that controlled the occupied area and whose prime motive was to achieve Japanese national and military goals.[5]

Most accounts of the film industry in wartime Japan available to English-language readers tend to homogenize the Japanese cinema in that period.[6] The war pictures of the late 1930s have been used to illustrate the formal and cultural difference of Japanese cinema, by contrasting it with American counterparts from Hollywood. However, these accounts have tended to ignore other popular genres, such as the home-front propaganda film and, most markedly, the interracial romance. The home-front type tends to be subsumed under studies of the work of the great Japanese film masters (Yasujiro Ozu, Akira Kurosawa, and Kenji Mizoguchi), which argue for the survival of distinctive authorial codes despite accommodation to wartime ideologies.[7] Indeed, the interracial romance film genre is often overlooked altogether.[8]

Like genre films, the star syndrome has received scant attention. Writers cling tenaciously to a director-centered view, focusing more on the aesthetic qualities rather than the more mundane production aspects of the industry. Generally, they ignore the fact that the Japanese film industry, like Hollywood, wooed audiences through genre specialization (as well as genre diversification) and the star system and that the great master directors were trained and worked in an industry in which production, distribution, exhibition, and promotion were based primarily on these categories.

Film and the Battlefront

Military-intelligence analysts in Washington observed, with some surprise, that Japanese combat films were more "realistic, presenting life as it is, an often unpleasant business, instead of glossing over the unpleasant aspects." They gave as an example the treatment of soldiers' lives: "full of mud, marching and misery as well as honorable service of their country." The American analysts concluded that the Japanese films and their audiences had a fatalistic attitude.[9]

Americans who were shown the Japanese films were astonished by such a dismal portrayal of combat and army life, according to anthropologist Ruth Benedict, who reported in 1946 that these viewers thought them to be "the best pacifist propaganda they ever saw." Benedict, who studied the culture in both Japan and America, concluded:

> [T]he movies are wholly concerned with the sacrifice and suffering of war. They do not play up military parades and bands and prideful showings of fleet manoevres or big guns. Whether they deal with the Russo-Japanese War or the China Incident, they starkly insist upon the monotonous routine of mud and marching, the sufferings of lowly fighting, the inconclusiveness of campaigns. Their curtain scenes are not victory or even *banzai* charges. They are overnight halts in some featureless Chinese town deep in mud. . . . Or they show the family at home, after the death of a soldier, mourning the loss of husband and father and breadwinner and gathering themselves together to go on without him. The stirring background of Anglo-American "Cavalcade" movies is absent. They do not even dramatize the theme of rehabilitation of wounded veterans. Not even the purposes for which the war was fought are mentioned.[10]

Film scholar Noel Burch has endorsed Benedict's observations and gone even further: "[I]n these films, war is always shown as a collective endeavour, in which individual personalities are totally submerged: Not only are there no heroes, but there are practically no characters."[11] Burch singles out two war films for close analysis: *Five Scouts* (Japan, 1938) and

Mud and Soldiers (Japan, 1939). He claims them to be representative of films of the period in their austerity and lack of characterization and close-ups. Formally, these Japanese combat films are closer to the newsreel than to the dramatic feature. Consisting primarily of long shots, they present, in Burch's words, "a collective hero surpassing even those of the Soviet silent cinema." Although "not entirely devoid of pathos," they place the dramatic emphasis on "the tragic absurdities of the situation," rather than on "the soldier's heroic generosity."[12]

A similar concentration on war movies is observable in the work of the Japanese film critic Tadeo Sato in his discussion of what he calls Japan's national policy films. But in creating a single all-encompassing genre, Sato fails to distinguish among the war film, the home-front propaganda picture, and the interracial romance.[13]

John Dower, a cultural historian of U.S.–Japanese relations, has argued that the purpose of Tokyo's domestic propaganda was to "spiritually mobilize the Japanese for a protracted conflict,"[14] and he concurs with Sato's view that war was represented as a kind of spiritual training, as a means of purifying the self. Seeking to explain why there are comparatively few caricatures of the enemy in Japanese wartime film propaganda as a whole, he offers the view that Japanese racism was less concerned with the denigration of others than with the elevation of themselves, with affirming their status as an allegedly superior and chosen people.[15]

However, Dower questions the true extent of the "realism" of Japan's war movies in the broader sense. He points to three major ideological omissions: the absence of physical brutality and mental abuse in military training; the absence of representations of the Japanese as victimizers; and the absence of the real Chinese war experience and suffering.[16]

Gender, Historical Accuracy, and the War Film

Gender does not figure as an issue in these analyses of the Japanese war movie.[17] The analysts fail to note that Tokyo's war films differ from their Hollywood counterparts not only in their generally more "realistic" representation of the life of soldiers but also in the absence of heterosexual romance. Especially in *The Story of Tank Commander Nishizumi* (Japan, 1940), the military unit is transformed into a surrogate family, with the emperor as father, the unit commander as caring mother, and the soldiers as loving brothers. The live body of so much as a single woman is absent. A brief glimpse of a photograph of a soldier's mother or wife is introduced sparingly either just before or just after his death in battle to add a touch of pathos to the event.

Commentators on Japanese wartime films also fail to historicize the genre accurately. Their observations describe a cycle of late-1930s motion pictures, major examples of which are *Five Scouts, Mud and Soldiers,* and *The Story of Tank Commander Nishizumi.* All of these were made *after* the 1937 invasion of China, which encountered unexpectedly heavy resistance and did not produce the decisive military victory expected by the Japanese militarists. The films were made, however, *before* the successful naval attack on Pearl Harbor and the spectacular victories by the Japanese army in southeast Asia.

After December 7, 1941, Japan widened the war dramatically to include the Pacific and Southeast Asia and began the total mobilization of industry (including the film sector) in support of the expanded effort. Thus increasingly between 1942 and 1945, the Japanese war film employed nationalist and militarist rhetoric—military parades, flag waving, aggressive-defensive arguments for the conflict, and stirring sequences of naval and air formations—that had been absent from the war films of the late 1930s. Although *Army* (Japan, 1944) has a profoundly disturbing finale that dramatizes the conflict between maternal desire and militarist nationalism, most of the picture makes strident use of nationalist, imperialist, and militarist rhetoric. Similarly, *Mother of the Sea* (Japan, 1942) concludes with a stirring image of the glorious Japanese navy sailing off to battle. Many of these post–Pearl Harbor films were made with the cooperation of the war ministries. They included parade-ground drills, formations of planes flying, battleships steaming, and enthusiastic crowds of children and civilians waving national flags as well as offering farewells to their military heroes. Saluting, marching, and singing of nationalistic songs are also typical.

Generally, however, wartime films posit the army unit and the nation as an extended family, or surrogate family, to replace the biological family. The Japanese were encouraged to view all other Japanese as brothers and sisters, as members of the same family. All personal relationships, including those among real family members, were to be subordinated to national service. Romantic love and even family affection had to be repressed in these films of national unity.

In the home-front propaganda films, children and parents, women and men, are all instructed in the military arts and virtues. In the extolling of the "Japanese spirit," gender difference and sexuality are played down.

The Japanese woman is required to be strong: to repress her femininity, her sexuality, her maternal affections, her personal desires and feelings. The teary excesses of the woman's melodrama and the joking playfulness of the domestic home-drama genre are deemed both inappropriate and unpatriotic in the serious wartime climate. So both of these popular genres were adapted to the ideology of asceticism.

China Nights: Interracial Wartime Romance Genre

If women are largely absent from the Japanese war film, and romance is largely absent from the home-front propaganda picture (because romance was deemed too trivial and decadent for wartime exigencies), both come into focus in another contemporary genre: the interracial romance. Here we find a use of romantic song and melodrama in marked contrast to the austerity, the repression, the gray uniformity of other wartime genres. The cycle of films in this genre was roughly contemporary with the war film. It began with *Song of the White Orchid* (Japan, 1939), which was followed by *China Nights* (Japan, 1940), *Vow in the Desert* (Japan, 1941), *Suchow Nights* (Japan, 1941), and *Fighting Street* (Japan, 1942).

The ideological function of the interracial romance genre was to transform the reality of Japanese armed aggression against China into a love story. The idea was to produce a national fantasy that substituted for the brutal military subjugation of the Chinese people a model of subjugation that was then socially and morally acceptable in Japan: marriage. Like the husband's view of the subordinated wife, the interracial romance film suggested that the relationship between Japan and China was one of paternal caring and protection. In this view, the Chinese had not been brutally subdued and subjugated; the Japanese were shown as loving them, caring for them, and guiding them. Consequently, the Chinese were portrayed as exhibiting in return love, respect, and appreciation for the guidance from Japan. This fantasy was avidly consumed by Japanese audiences who found it much more palatable to believe the Chinese had been subdued by love and superior Japanese virtues than by brute force and naked power. (Of course, such a portrayal also concurred with official pan-Asianism and the rhetoric of interracial harmony in the Greater East-Asian Co-Prosperity Sphere, wartime Japan's term for its conquered empire.)

Interracial romance in film and literature has often functioned as a palliative for the qualms of oppressors, by replacing hard-core racism with soft-core sentimentality. Not coincidentally, it normally involves a romance between a man of the imperial or dominant race and a woman of the colonized or subordinate race. It thus neatly collapses the politics of gender into the politics of race and disavows both in the construction of the fantasy of transcendent romantic love.

This genre also functioned as an emotional release from the ideology of asceticism, by offering Japanese audiences indulgence in an otherwise taboo romantic fantasy, a flirtation with the foreign, the feminine, the uncivilized. It also provided an alternative to that repressive puritanical machine of the nonindividualized, noncentered, nonheroic, underdramatized Japanese cinema. In the interracial genre, Japanese filmmakers could draw on Hollywood-style cinema.

China Nights (Shina no Yoru)[18] is "the great classic" of the whole genre, and "possibly the most shameless and fascinating propaganda exercise of the war years," according to Dower.[19] The film is a romantic melodrama set in late 1930s China that focuses on the romantic relationship between a handsome Japanese naval officer and a beautiful young Chinese woman. Produced by the Toho film company and directed by a B-grade director, Osamu Fushimizu, the 126-minute picture stars Kazuo Hasegawa, a matinee idol who had been the star romantic lead for the period melodramas produced by the competing Shochiku company.

For the feminine lead, the studio selected Ri Ko Ran (the Japanese version of her Chinese name, Li Hsiang-Lan), who had been a singer and star of Man-Ei, the Japanese-run Manchurian Film Company, which had been set up in the late 1930s to provide entertainment and "edification" for the population of the conquered province of Manchuria. *China Nights* proved to be the biggest hit ever produced by the Toho studios, and Japanese film historian Junichiro Tanaka attributes its success to the popularity of exotic Chinese locations and to the sensational popularity of Ri Ko Ran with Japanese audiences at this time.[20]

Released in 1940, the film had been shot and set in 1939 in the war-ravaged city of Shanghai. That major Chinese port and industrial city had been invaded from the sea by Japanese forces. It had been conquered only after several months of savage fighting between August and November 1937. The shattered ruins of the Chinese section of the city that had experienced heavy air and naval bombardment during the Japanese offensive in 1937 are evident in parts of the film.

In the opening of *China Nights*, Hase, a Japanese naval officer (played by Hasegawa) intercedes in an unpleasant incident in the streets of Shanghai, then occupied by Japanese forces. A lower-class Japanese man

Shanghai, 1939: Japanese naval officer, played by Kazuo Hasegawa, woos beautiful young Chinese war orphan in traditional Chinese garb, played by Ri Ko Ran, in *China Nights* (Japan, 1940). (Personal collection of the author)

and, Keiran-chi, a dirty, homeless Chinese girl (played by Ri Ko Ran) are trading insults, following the man's attempt to harass her. Afterward, in order to correct the girl's bad impression of the Japanese, the officer invites her to live in his Japanese-owned hotel. Despite her dirty appearance, her defiant attitude, and her rough and rude manner, the orphaned street child is welcomed into the hotel by kind and cultured Japanese women who lavish sympathy and reforming zeal on her (in the manner of noblesse oblige). With more than a hint of Eliza Doolittle in the hands of Professor Henry Higgins, the initially resistant Ri Ko Ran endures the ignominy of being bathed and cleaned and coddled and dressed. When she becomes seriously ill with fever, she is nursed back to health with great loving care by the naval officer. When she still resists his kindness, he succeeds by disciplinary measures (including sharp words and a slap) to reeducate her into loving and respecting him.

Although she has now succumbed to love, an external obstacle to the couple's union emerges. Her anti-Japanese cousin objects to their relationship and arranges for her abduction by his underworld gang (in these

Japanese melodramas, anti-Japanese Chinese are usually represented as bandits, rather than Nationalists or Communists). The naval officer follows them to their hideaway and rescues Ri Ko Ran in a Hollywood-style shoot-out. After this ordeal, the two declare their love for each other and vacation in Soochow, where they enjoy a romantic idyll and become engaged. She now speaks fluent Japanese and behaves like a well-mannered and demure Japanese lady. In one final trial of her new identity, she loses her bridegroom to military duty on their wedding night. She prays for his safe return. When he seems to have been lost, she is willing to follow him in death, like a good Japanese wife. She is about to commit suicide by drowning when he makes a dramatic return, alive though wounded. She is overjoyed. They return to the site of their romantic idyll in Soochow. The film ends as they embrace to the rising strains of the theme song.

It is easy to mock this melodrama for its imperialist politics and Hollywood-style aesthetics. In substantiation of the latter, one must note

Now dressed in modern Japanese clothing, the young Chinese woman has accepted the culture as well as the marriage proposal of her Japanese suitor, dining in civilian clothes, in *China Nights* (Japan, 1940). (Personal collection of the author)

the saccharine romantic theme song,[21] constantly heard throughout the film; the centering of the narrative on the relationship between the heterosexual couple; and the representation of the demonstration of the development of that relationship through an exchange of heavily charged looks. As for the politics, the obvious meaning has been noted by film scholars Joseph Anderson and Donald Richie: "Japan was rescuing China from, among other things, the perils of communism. The two were to live in peaceful co-prosperity ever after."[22] Indeed, such was the official propaganda line of Japanese imperialism: Pan-Asianism under Japanese direction as an alternative to anarchic communism or Western imperialism. Its propaganda message is why the movie has been termed a "national-policy film." More interestingly, the marriage between the two leading characters signifies "virile Japan happily bedded with weak effeminate China."[23]

Although historically China had sometimes been regarded as the aged parent of younger Japan, or perhaps its older brother, in *China Nights* such a relationship is reversed. China becomes the child who must be disciplined and reformed by paternal Japan, and even transformed into the image of Japan.

A problem relating to gender remains. If films like *China Nights* function to confirm the gender, as well as the national/racial superiority, of the male subject, how can one explain their popularity with female spectators? For wartime Japanese viewers, it was an outlet for emotional indulgence not permitted in pictures with local settings. Japanese women were supposed to be stoic, enduring, strong, like their menfolk; women were warriors on the home front; romance was an indulgence that was inappropriate in wartime. Perhaps identification with the weak, feminine, Chinese urchin offered a masochistic fantasy that relieved Japanese women of the weight of the responsibilities placed on them, but allowed them to disavow that identification (perhaps thinking that, after all, she's a weak Chinese, a foreigner). As a Japanese national, though, a female spectator in Japan could also identify with the Japanese male hero, and with the imperialist ideology of national pride, power, and paternalism.

China Nights is interesting to us today not only as an example of wartime Japanese Orientalism. It can also be said to complicate the debate about the meaning of cultural identity—and even cross-dressing. For the actress playing the Chinese collaborationist heroine, known as Ri Ko Ran to the Japanese and as Li Hsiang-Lan to the Chinese, was, although indeed a woman, not really Chinese. She was an ethnic Japanese from Manchuria named Yoshiko Yamaguchi. Since she publicly posed as Chinese, while actually being Japanese, she was in fact a Chinese impersonator, dressing the part in Chinese clothing. This knowledge, not available to her wartime audiences, helps to make the film all the more interesting. If gender-bending cross-dressing in the theater and the cinema can be said to call into question and unsettle gender categories, then cross-dressing over national and racial lines can be said to call into question and unsettle national and racial categories.

Nevertheless, if young Yoshiko Yamaguchi, who went by the double stage names of Li Hsiang-Lan (in China) and Ri Ko Ran (in Japan), could convince Chinese and Japanese audiences that she was Chinese—by donning a cheongsam, speaking and singing in Chinese, and using a Chinese name—then it does suggest that, contrary to Japanese nationalistic belief, there is no essential difference between a Chinese and a Japanese woman. Adding to the ambiguity, her co-star Hasegawa (who played the naval officer in *China Nights*) had originally been a female impersonator on the kabuki stage before he became a film actor and a leading male star.[24] In *China Nights,* Hasegawa coached Ri Ko Ran into giving a more moving and more convincingly feminine performance for this romantic melodrama.

Shifting Identities of the Female Star

The fame of Ri Ko Ran went beyond *China Nights;* she became the star of the whole interracial romance genre in Japanese cinema. We now know a great deal more about her than did the audiences of wartime Japan.[25] She was born Yoshiko Yamaguchi in Fushun, Manchuria, in 1920, the daughter of Japanese settlers there. Her father was a China expert employed by the Japanese-run South Manchurian Railways (Mantetsu); he had studied in Beijing and had a circle of Chinese friends who were useful to Japan and who were branded as collaborators after the war. Young Yoshiko went to school with Chinese and Russian girls and studied classical Western singing under an Italian music teacher married to a White Russian aristocrat. Yoshiko appears to have been bilingual, if not trilingual. As a teenager, she gave recitals of Japanese and Russian songs. While still a schoolgirl, she was enlisted to sing Chinese songs on the radio in Mukden, a provincial capital in Manchuria. She took the stage name of Li Hsiang Lan (probably from a General Li who was a close friend of her father and was possibly her godfather).

When the Japanese-run Man-Ei film company in Manchuria decided to produce a series of musicals and other light-entertainment films for the Chinese population, they invited young Yoshiko Yamaguchi to join them; they also wanted her to maintain her Chinese alias. The commercial success of Man-Ei was reputedly based on her popularity and led to her being hired by the Toho motion picture company in Japan. As Ri Ko Ran, she achieved spectacular success in Japan as a stage singer, a recording star, and a film star. She served the Japanese war effort by playing the role of a beautiful Chinese girl—she always dressed in Chinese clothing for public appearances—who was the seductive and accommodating collaborator of the Japanese. Between a hectic schedule of film shootings in Japan and on the Asian mainland, as well as concert appearances and recording studio sessions, she also entertained Japanese troops at the front.

In her postwar career, she never recaptured her wartime success. After 1945, she abandoned her Chinese persona and resumed the use of her birth name, Yoshiko Yamaguchi, and a public identity as ethnic Japanese. Her subsequent career in the film industry in Japan was undistinguished. She came to the United States by invitation in 1950. Under the name of Shirley Yamaguchi, she starred in a Broadway production of *Shangri-La,* and then in Hollywood played the role of a Japanese woman in two American films: *Japanese War Bride* (U.S., 1952) and *House of Bamboo* (U.S., 1955). In the latter, her role seems no more than a perfunctory nod at Hollywood structures—the obligatory inclusion of heterosexual romance. The real emotional center of *House of Bamboo* is the relationship between two men: Robert Stack and Robert Ryan. Still, it is revealing that in postwar Hollywood, as in wartime Japan, she was cast in interracial romances; the despised but redeemable Chinese street urchin of the Japanese occupation of China became the despised but redeemable "kimono girl" of the American military occupation of Japan.

She returned to Japan and continued to have film roles there until 1958, when she married a Japanese diplomat and retired from the motion-picture industry. In the 1970s, when she was in her fifties, she worked as a television journalist. Under her married name of Yoshiko Otaka, she was elected a member of the Upper House of the Japanese national legislature, the Diet, in 1974 and has continued to serve in that capacity ever since. Her autobiography, *Ri Ko Ran: Watashi no Hansei* [The First Half of My Life], was published in 1987.[26]

The most popular film genre in wartime Japan—the interracial romance—and Ri Ko Ran, its sensationally popular star, have been neglected by scholars of Japanese cinema for rather obvious reasons. Because these films were not directed by the great masters of the Japanese cinema, and because they do not exhibit marked formal or cultural difference, they do not fit the dominant agendas of Western scholarship on Japanese motion pictures. This body of scholarship generally concentrates on the art film and the avant-garde.

In the process, however, such scholarship neglects—indeed, often disdains—Japanese film audiences and popular culture, especially female audiences and genres.[27] Clearly, too, such wartime pictures today are a source of embarrassment to national pride in both Japan and China. As rather crass examples of Japanese propaganda, exhibiting insulting attitudes toward the Chinese, they are discomforting reminders of a past that today many in the two nations would rather forget. This amnesia, denial, even censorship of the past, including the film history of the wartime era, has enabled the Japanese to continue to represent themselves as victims, to deny their actual role as conquerers and oppressors of the Chinese people.

Some students of Japanese history, such as John Dower and William Hauser, have in the 1990s pointed to certain troubling continuities between the wartime Japanese cinema (by which they mean the home-front propaganda film and the war pictures) and the postwar Japanese motion-picture industry.[28] In particular, these scholars point to the filmic representation of the Japanese experience of the war. Dower finds troubling the way in which the Japanese continued to represent themselves simply as victims rather than as actively responsible for their actions. The sources of evil and corruption may have shifted to new targets, but the attitude has remained the same. Hauser bemoans the continuing confinement of the role of Japanese women to the realm of the family, and their exclusion from the political arena.

In the mid-1950s, after the end of the American occupation of Japan, a number of elegiac films were produced, mourning the loss of life and liberty during the war. *Harp of Burma* (Japan, 1956) is a wrenching film that made a major impact with film-festival audiences around the world; it represented the ordinary Japanese soldier as a tragic victim of war, rather than as an active participant in the brutality of the conquest. Both *Children of Hiroshima* (Japan, 1953) and *24 Eyes* (Japan, 1954) present the experience of the war through the eyes of a female teacher who, like a good mother, empathizes with the suffering of her children. But like the obedient citizen, she stands by as the children are maimed and killed in the cruel war. The soft, sorrowing treatment is affecting, but ultimately not very effective as social criticism.

A harsher and more critical view of the Japanese engagement in the war is offered by Masaki Kobayashi in his powerful trilogy *The Human Condition* (Japan, 1958–1961), which describes the wartime career of Kaji, a pacifist Japanese soldier who experiences one horror after another. These films do present the brutal exploitation of Chinese labor by the occupying Japanese forces, the viciousness of Japanese military training, and the general collapse of all civilized values in wartime. In the end, the hero, despite his strong personality and very modern moral conscience, becomes yet another war victim, suffering horribly in every conceivable disaster.

As Japanese critic Inuhiko Yomota has suggested, an analysis of the Ri Kō Ran phenomenon is long overdue.[29] The convenient national neglect of Japan's imperialist cinema has allowed the Japanese to persist in representing themselves as innocent victims, to maintain an attitude of self-righteousness. By failing to face up to the racism and sexism that underpinned their imperialist cinema, they have indulged in an exercise in national self-denial—an action that Yomota darkly alleges is a cover-up for unchanged national attitudes.

NOTES

The author would like to acknowledge the help she received from Sachiko Noguchi and Hisako Sato in locating and/or translating Japanese materials.

1. Chinese historians generally refer to this as the Sino-Japanese War of 1931 or 1937 to 1945; postwar Japanese favor the term Pacific War. Because there seems to be no satisfactory solution to the problem of naming the wars in the East between 1931 and 1945, it is convenient to fall back on the term World War II, even though it is not really an appropriate or entirely accurate designation.

2. Copies of the Japanese motion pictures of the war and prewar periods (245 feature films in all), along with a large number of captured Japanese wartime newsreels, are available for use by researchers at the Motion Picture, Broadcasting, and Recorded Sound Division of the Library of Congress, Washington, D.C.

3. U.S., Office of Strategic Services, Research and Analysis Branch, "Japanese Films: A Phase of Psychological Warfare," report no. 1307, March 30, 1944, 097.3, Z1092, no. 1307R; OSS, R&A Branch, "Public Information in Japan," report no. 2362, August 20, 1945, 097.3, Z1092, no. 2362R, in OSS Records, National Archives, Washington, D.C.

4. Tadao Sato, "Japanese War Films," in *Currents in Japanese Cinema* (Toyko: Kodansha International; New York: Kodansha International/Harper & Row, 1982);

Joseph Anderson and Donald Richie, "Shooting Script: 1939–45," in their *The Japanese Film: Art and Industry,* rev. ed. (Princeton: Princeton University Press, 1982); Joan Mellen, "The Japanese Film During the Second World War," in her *The Waves at Genji's Door: Japan Through Its Cinema* (New York: Pantheon Books, 1976).

5. Kyoko Hirano notes the "strange mixture of ideological orientations unique to Japanese-occupied Manchuria" among the Japanese staff at Man-Ei, the Japanese-run Manchurian Film Company (*Mr. Smith Goes to Tokyo: The Japanese Cinema Under the American Occupation, 1945–1952* [Washington D.C.: Smithsonian Institution Press, 1992], pp. 117–18). See also Stefan Tanaka, *Japan's Orient: Rendering Pasts into History* (Berkeley: University of California Press, 1993), p. 259. For accounts of the trials and tribulations of Nagamasa Kawakita, a liberal Japanese Sinophile who ran the film industry in Shanghai under the Japanese Occupation, see Akira Shimizu, "President Kawakita and Chinese Film," in *Towa Eiga no Ayumi: 1928–1955* (The Progress of Towa Film Company: 1928–1955) (Tokyo: Towa Films Pty [*sic*], 1955), pp. 294–302.

6. Major surveys of Japanese cinema, which include discussions of the wartime cinema, are Sato, *Currents in Japanese Cinema;* Anderson and Richie, *Japanese Film;* Mellen, *Waves at Genji's Door;* and Noel Burch, *To the Distant Observer: Form and Meaning in the Japanese Cinema* (London: Scholar Press, 1979).

7. See, for example, Stephen Prince, *The Warrior's Camera: The Cinema of Akira Kurosawa* (Princeton: Princeton University Press, 1991).

8. Mellen, "Japanese Film During the Second World War," and Burch, *To the Distant Observer,* entirely neglect the interracial-romance film genre, while Anderson and Richie, "Shooting Script," subsume it under the category of "national policy films with Chinese settings." Japanese critic Tadao Sato, in "Japanese War Films," connects it suggestively with postwar Hollywood interracial romances like *The Teahouse of the August Moon* (U.S., 1956) and *Sayonara* (U.S., 1957) in his discussion of the so-called *rashamen* (Japanese–Western romance) genre of the 1950s. See also John Dower, "Japanese Cinema Goes to War," in his *Japan in War and Peace: Selected Essays* (New York: New Press, 1993), pp. 33–54.

9. OSS, R&A Branch, "Public Information in Japan."

10. Ruth Benedict, *The Chrysanthemum and the Sword: Patterns of Japanese Culture* (1946; New York: Meridian, 1967), pp. 193–94.

11. Burch, *To the Distant Observer,* p. 263.

12. Ibid., p. 268.

13. Sato, "Japanese War Films," pp. 103–4.

14. John Dower, *War Without Mercy: Race and Power in the Pacific War* (New York: Pantheon Books, 1986), p. 206.

15. Ibid., pp. 204–5.

16. Dower, "Japanese Cinema Goes to War," pp. 50–51.

17. Gender does not emerge as an issue in Dower's major study of wartime propaganda, *War Without Mercy.*

18. *China Nights* (Shina no Yoru) (Toho Film Company, 1940), 126 minutes. Osamu Fushimizu, director; Hideo Oguni, screenplay; Takashi Matsuyama, cinematography; Ryoichi Hattori, music, with songs sung by Hamako Watanabe. A 16-mm copy in Japanese, without English subtitles, is located in the Motion Picture, Broadcasting, and Recorded Sound Division of the Library of Congress, Washington, D.C.

19. Dower, "Japanese Cinema Goes to War," p. 46.

20. Junichiro Tanaka, *Nihon Eiga Hattatsu Shi* (Developmental History of Japanese Film) (Tokyo: Chuei Koron, 1976), vol. 3, p. 45.

21.
> China Nights. China Nights.
> Harbor Lights. Purple Nights.
> Sailboats in a dream. Sailing in the night.
> Ohhhh. . . . The lingering strains of the guitar strings.
> China Nights. Dreamy Nights.

22. Anderson and Richie, "Shooting Script," p. 155.

23. Ibid.

24. Kazuo Hasegawa was born in 1908, trained as a female impersonator (*onnagata*) in kabuki performances, and started his motion-picture career in 1927. He was the star of period melodramas produced by the Shochiku studio until 1937, when he was hired away by Toho, a rival company. Shochiku was so angered by his defection (and the loss of their biggest period star) that they hired a gangster to punish him by slashing his face.

25. See, for example, Freda Freiberg, "Ri Ko Ran/Shirley Yamaguchi," in *Dictionary of the Cinema,* ed. Geoffrey Nowell-Smith (Oxford: Oxford University Press, forthcoming).

26. Most of the biographical details are derived from her autobiography, *Ri Ko Ran: Watashi no Hansei* (Tokyo: Shincho Press, 1987). For a more inflammatory account of her career, see Ian Buruma, "Haunted Heroine," *Interview,* September 1989, pp. 124–27. The Hong Kong Film Festival, in conjunction with a Ri Ko Ran retrospective in 1992, published *Hong Kong Film Festival Ri Ko Ran Retrospective Catalogue* (in Chinese), with film credits of the productions in which she performed.

27. There are signs that things are changing; see Miriam Silverberg, "Remembering Pearl Harbour, Forgetting Charlie Chaplin and the Case of the Disappearing Western Woman: A Picture Story," *Positions: east asia cultures critique* 1, no. 1 (1993): 24–76.

28. See William Hauser, "Women and War: The Japanese Film Image," in *Recreating Japanese Women, 1600–1945,* ed. Gail Lee Bernstein (Berkeley: University of California Press, 1991), pp. 312–13; and Dower, *Japan in War and Peace,* p. 50.

29. Inuhiko Yomota, "Ri Ko Ran—Daughter of the Occupied Territory," in *Hong Kong Film Festival Ri Ko Ran Retrospective Catalogue.*

3

Kolberg (Germany, 1945):
As Historical Film
and Historical Document

PETER PARET

Kolberg (Germany, 1945) is not among the major successes of the German motion-picture industry during the Third Reich. It achieved coherence neither as a drama nor—despite its excess of rhetorical energy—as a political statement. Nevertheless, the film continues to attract attention. The circumstances of its production, its aesthetic qualities and flaws, and its evidentiary power as a document of the last phase of National Socialism at war—all serve to keep interest alive in a work in which Goebbels, and through him the regime, invested material resources and psychic expectations to an unusual degree.

The literature on *Kolberg* remains, however, uneven and fragmentary. Aspects of the script have been subjected to close analysis, but the script and, indeed, the film as a whole have not yet received adequate treatment. Veit Harlan's direction and such important components of the work as Norbert Schultze's score, and its interaction with the film's images and their message, still await systematic study. Nor do we know enough about the making of the film, from inception to the final cut. The literature relies heavily on Harlan's memoirs, but he is a questionable witness even when his relationship to the regime is not at issue. His memoirs are enlightening about the life and work of a small, privileged group of film and theater people under National Socialism, but they mix up dates and confuse events. When he writes about *Kolberg,* he is often informative, sometimes ambiguous and hard to understand, and sometimes misleading—as when he claims that he employed 187,000 soldiers in making the film.[1]

Considering the nature of his memoirs, it is hardly surprising that Harlan even misquotes his own script.[2]

A further reason for the weakness of some discussions of *Kolberg* may at first seem surprising: the mistakes their authors make when they refer to the historical subject that forms the film's principal theme. Dramatic treatments of the past always compress, simplify, and intentionally or not falsify the historical evidence, and since the writer, the director, and their colleagues reshape the historical material, why should the later interpreter be concerned about getting the events right? But the interpreter of a film is not in the same position as its maker. To know such basic facts as names, chronology, and other items of record—to say nothing of interpretations, which may be complex and disputed—and compare them with their treatment in the film offer us a special perspective on the motives and attitudes of the filmmakers and their backers. We can then ask: What caused the scriptwriter or the director to reject historical truth? Getting the facts wrong ourselves, or being unaware of them, deprives us of a valuable interpretive tool.

A few examples will demonstrate the point. It is not correct to write that "in 1806 Prussia surrendered to France, a defeat which the film passes over in silence."[3] Had that been the case, Kolberg would not have been besieged in 1807 and the film, presumably, would not have been made. Nor is it true that in 1806, "only the fortress town of Kolberg prevented a complete victory for the French" or that "despite the Kolberger's courageous resistance they were eventually overwhelmed by the French."[4] The siege of Kolberg was a minor incident in the campaign of 1807, which included two battles with many thousands of casualties on both sides and any number of engagements and sieges, and the town remained in Prussian hands after the war.[5] The commandant of the fortress was never "determined to surrender without resistance." He was a conscientious, if not very imaginative, soldier—only the film transformed him into a reactionary bungler.[6]

To turn from Prussian history to the history of the film, Harlan did not assert that "Hitler and Goebbels were convinced that such a film [*Kolberg*] was more useful than a military victory."[7] The two men were not that foolish, and even Harlan never claimed that much power for his films. What he did was to speculate in his memoirs that in view of the resources committed to the project, "Hitler and Goebbels must have been possessed [*besessen,* demonized] by the thought that such a film might do them more good than, for instance, a victory in Russia," which is rather different. Harlan added, "Perhaps they were merely waiting for a miracle."[8] Schultze did not compose the nursery rhyme "Maikäfer flieg," which Kristina Söderbaum, who plays the heroine, sings in one of the stronger scenes of the film; verse and melody antedate the Third Reich by centuries.[9] Goebbels did not order Harlan to write a script that would "symbolize the continual conflict between the SA and the Waffen-SS, with the former depicted as the true heroes."[10] If true, this would have revealed a very odd view on Goebbels's part of the relations between the SA and the SS. In reality, Goebbels wanted the film to stress the conflict between traditional and revolutionary attitudes in 1807 as a way of symbolizing the rivalry between the SA and the SS, on the one hand, and the *Wehrmacht*, on the other.[11] Nor, finally, is it the case that the line from Theodor Körner's poem "Männer und Buben"—"The people rise, the storm erupts"—which serves as a key motif in the film, "became the slogan for the whole campaign [presumably of 1813] and gave rise to the name *Volkssturm* [people's storm] for the armed civilian militia raised by the Nazis to defend the Reich in its dying days."[12] The word *Sturm* in conjunction with *Volk* or *Land*, meaning "mobilization of the population for home defense," has a long history in central Europe. In 1813, Prussia adopted it from secret plans of 1808 for an uprising against the French and from the Tyrolean insurrection of 1809.

As the last two examples demonstrate with particular clarity, historical accuracy is not a pedantic quirk that analysts of *Kolberg* can afford to ignore. It affects the interpretation of the film itself as well as one's view of the film's place in its historical context. Körner did not invent the term *Volkssturm*, nor did the film reinvent it, and Harlan is undoubtedly correct when he writes that *Kolberg* was planned and produced too early for it to have been intended as a propaganda vehicle for the *Volkssturm* of 1945.[13] What is true, however, and far more interesting, is that a film conceived, written, and partly shot in 1943 closely fit the conditions and expressed certain attitudes of the early months of 1945. A good starting point for an inquiry into this relationship might be Goebbels's remark while the picture was being made that Kolberg "fits exactly the military and political landscape that we shall probably have to record by the time this film is shown."[14]

The following comments address some aspects of Prussian history and their restatement in the film. Comparing what actually happened in the past with the work's treatment of the past, and relating the film's content to the conditions in which it was made and shown, may contribute to a clearer understanding of its intentions and eventual message—what *Kolberg* really conveyed to its audience when it was released in January 1945.

The idea for the film originated during World War II, but its plot became compelling only when the Third Reich began to suffer setbacks. As the perimeter of Fortress Europe shrank, the subject presented itself as a parable of a nation that shakes off defeatism and disunity at home and thus overcomes terrible dangers from abroad.

The events that make the film topical are obvious. And yet the first few frames attempt to obscure one aspect of this link. The credits announce that the film is based on history, and—an unusual addition— that work on it began in 1942. In reality, Goebbels approved the project in the spring of 1943, and Harlan wrote the script and began shooting in September of that year. But evidently the Propaganda Ministry wanted the public to believe that the film was conceived earlier, that it was not a response to the disaster of Stalingrad, the defeat of the Afrika Korps, and the inability of the *Luftwaffe* to protect German cities against destruction from the air. The film was a call for total war, but it awkwardly—and perhaps as an afterthought—denied the crises that made total war necessary.

The historical facts to which the credits refer are drawn from the early nineteenth century. In the fall of 1806, Napoleon attacked Prussia, defeated its main armies, and occupied Berlin. Resistance continued in the eastern provinces, and it was only in June 1807, after hard fighting, that Prussia finally sued for peace. One of the places that was not immediately overrun was the small town of Kolberg on the Baltic coast. The commandant of the garrison, an old colonel who had been given this post in lieu of a pension, did what he could to prepare the town for a siege; but it was felt that someone more energetic was needed, and he was replaced. The new man, a Major Gneisenau, arrived in April 1807, took command of the garrison of 5,700 men, appealed to the burghers for help, and gained an important ally in the chairman of the town council, an old sea captain named Nettelbeck. For the next two months, soldiers and townspeople together defended Kolberg against a French force that eventually increased to 13,000 men.

Probably because Harlan and his co-workers knew that whatever figures were mentioned in the film would not be believed anyway, they made the French still stronger and the Prussians still weaker, until the relationship was 15 to 1. During the siege, the garrison and the town suffered more than 860 casualties, and many houses were destroyed, but Kolberg was still in Prussian hands when the war ended. For the French, the failure to take the town was a minor irritation; for the Prussians, it became a symbol, the more so since the siege was one of the rare instances in a disastrous war when civilians and regular soldiers joined to defend their country—a coming together reflective of values that were only beginning to replace the absolutist concepts of the ancien régime.

The siege had another effect as well: it made Gneisenau a major figure in Prussia. He became a leader in the reform of the army and state. After Napoleon's disaster in Russia, he helped persuade the Prussian king to turn against France, and as Blücher's chief of staff at Waterloo, he was one of the architects of Napoleon's ultimate defeat.

The defense of Kolberg forms the central plot of the film, and its relevance to Germany in retreat is obvious. As Goebbels wrote to Harlan when he commissioned the film, the purpose was to show that people united—battlefront and home front together—could overcome any opponent.[15] The film relates the defense of the town in a single long flashback, which at the beginning and end is framed by explanations of the historical and current significance of Kolberg's martyrdom. These framing scenes outline the conflict over Prussian policy in 1813, in which Gneisenau points to the siege six years earlier to show what patriotism can achieve.

It is not surprising that Harlan compressed the complex and drawn-out process by which Prussia reentered the war against France into a confrontation between the hesitant king and the fiery, idealistic Gneisenau. But one particular historical correction gives us a clue to the film's underlying ideology. In 1813, the real Gneisenau was in his early fifties, ten years older than the king. In the film, Harlan made the king the older man, cautious and anxious, while Gneisenau was played as a dynamic thirty-year-old. Harlan's falsification underlines the film's central argument: in the crisis in which the Third Reich finds itself, traditional ways of thinking and acting must be scrapped. Germans must renounce old standards and assumptions. They must follow the leadership of a young, revolutionary movement—a new order.

The didactic beginning and ending that frame the film demonstrate the contemporary significance of Kolberg's defense. According to Harlan, they were conceived by Goebbels, who, by effectively fusing past and present, made the costume drama a part of the German reality of the

At the beginning and again at the end of the film *Kolberg* (Germany, 1945), Prussian soldiers and civilians in 1813 demonstrate their eagerness to rise up against Napoleon. Their patriotism has been inspired by such episodes as the defense of Kolberg against the French six years earlier. (Frame enlargement by Gerhard Ullmann)

1940s. This was achieved not only by means of images. The film's musical theme turns a patriotic poem written in 1813 by the young poet Theodor Körner into a revolutionary anthem sung by massed troops at the film's beginning and climax. The soldiers are shown in the fatigue caps that the Prussian army introduced in 1813, which providentially bear a slight resemblance to the cloth caps of the SA and other Nazi organizations. But Körner's line "Das Volk steht auf, der Sturm bricht los" was also chosen by Goebbels (the wording somewhat changed, as was his wont) as the end of one of his most important and widely discussed speeches during the war—his response to the disaster of Stalingrad, in which he proclaimed total war.[16] And the film's musical setting of the line, its musical leit-motif, recalls the *Horst Wessel Song,* the marching song of the SA, not structurally but in its rhetorical gesture, the melody punctuated by pauses filled with the sound of marching feet. Only now the song's combative optimism has been transposed into an apocalyptic chant, which hints that 1945 is no longer 1933, and gives us yet another clue to the film's ultimate message.[17]

But the main part of the picture presented Harlan with a basic problem: Could an extended military episode with ideological overtones, undiluted by romance, have audience appeal? Goebbels instructed Harlan to add a love interest, a solution that accorded fully with Harlan's general outlook. He invented a subplot, centered on a young woman, which allowed him to introduce a love story and to show the effects of the war on one family, whose members react in different ways to the fighting. Very likely, this broadened audience appeal. The romance between a young, idealistic girl and a dynamic, self-willed officer, which ends in renunciation for the sake of the fatherland, but also because the soldier prefers the masculine world of fighting to a settled family life, was a romantic cliché, familiar to the audience from any number of earlier films. The subplot was the sugar that helped the medicine go down, and the filmic

Lieutenant von Schill drills volunteers in the Kolberg town square. (Frame enlargement by Gerhard Ullmann)

Nettelbeck persuades his fellow councillors to oppose the French rather than surrender. (Frame enlargement by Gerhard Ullmann)

convention of youth, opulent uniforms, and sex appeal easily became a vehicle for propaganda.

The love story not only offered the audience something it liked and was accustomed to see, and thus made it more receptive to the rest of the film, it also developed its own political message. By making the girl the town's emissary to the government, braving the hazardous journey from Kolberg to Königsberg to beg for a new, enterprising commandant, and by having her appeal not to the king or a senior officer but to another woman, the queen, the film declares that women do more than wait and endure while their men fight—they have an active role to play. When men marvel at the girl's courage in risking the trip, she answers, "A woman can do such things." Toward the end of the film, she is assured by Nettelbeck, the man who inspired Kolberg to resist, "You are great, Maria . . . you, too, have triumphed, Maria. You too."

The basic scheme of the subplot shows a sophisticated political intelligence at work; the conventional romantic melodrama passes on worn-out ideological messages as easily as it conveys unrealistic images of feelings and actions. But the plot's implementation does not match the simplicity of its message. It is needlessly complex, and often poorly integrated with the main subject. Further, the sentimental, artificial style of acting that characterizes most scenes clashes with the fighting episodes, which attempt to treat battle and the destruction and survival of the town in a more realistic manner, and this disparity contributes to the unevenness that mars the work as a whole.

Among the feeble and stilted scenes, a few strong episodes stand out. In what are perhaps the best six minutes of the film, the town council discusses the French demand to surrender before the siege begins. This episode is followed by its counterpart, a shorter, also effective scene in which Napoleon gives the order to eliminate the nuisance of a free Kolberg, and to take the town by storm. The council meeting in Kolberg introduces the viewer to strong and weak types—among the latter an intellectual and a capitalist—all dominated by the powerful personality of Chairman Nettelbeck, who is played by one of the outstanding actors of the Weimar period and the Third Reich, Heinrich George. In preparing the defense of the town and in the fighting itself, Nettelbeck, who is shown as a man of middle age or older, is the junior partner to the far younger Gneisenau. But although it is the young officer who leads, it is

French troops advance on the town. (Frame enlargement by Gerhard Ullmann)

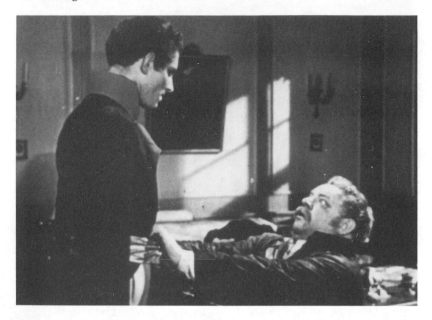

To test Nettelbeck's determination, the new commandant, Gneisenau, tells him that the town cannot be held. Nettelbeck passes the test by begging him never to surrender. (Frame enlargement by Gerhard Ullmann)

the partnership between youth and age, soldier and civilian, that is the decisive point. Once again, the film brings past and present together, this time by emphasizing George's physical similarity to the aged Field Marshal Hindenburg, a man who for many Germans symbolized absolute rectitude and who in 1933 had called on Hitler to assume the post of chancellor.[18]

The glittering scene in Napoleon's headquarters serves to highlight the admirable qualities revealed in the preceding discussion among down-to-earth German merchants and sailors. Not only are the French aggressors and the Prussian victims of aggression contrasted, but also Napoleonic autocracy with the burghers of Kolberg, who like the members of an old Germanic tribe reach the ultimate decisions of life and death through debate and the willing subordination to an inspired leader. The French generals and Napoleon himself are treated with some sympathy or at least detachment; but the emperor's promise to make the conqueror of Kolberg a duke—a motivation that plays a role later on—introduces yet another contrast, that between the patriotic Germans and their mercenary, selfish enemies.

The scenes of combat form the most unusual part of the film. In his memoirs, Harlan prides himself on their historical accuracy as well as their impressive imagery and dramatic power.[19] In reality, they are a director's fantasy. The fighting around Kolberg in 1807 consisted largely of the attack and defense of small fortified positions; of night raids, ambushes, and sniping; and of hand-to-hand combat in the ditches and trenches with which the attackers and defenders encircled the town. None of that is in the film, which depicts the siege as a battle of huge units, moving in geometric patterns until they are smashed by enemy fire, or of vast mobs rushing back and forth across a cinematic landscape that has been deprived of any physical or moral point of reference.

The rejection of past reality continues in the most dramatic part of the siege—the shelling of the town. The power of the French cannon drawn up theatrically in an endless line, and the devastation they create, go beyond anything imaginable in the early nineteenth century, as Harlan

French infantry try but fail to advance through fields flooded by the townspeople. (Frame enlargement by Gerhard Ullmann)

Nettelbeck consoles Maria for the deaths of her father and brothers, and for the departure of Schill, the man she loves: "You stayed at your post and did your duty . . . you, too, have triumphed, Maria." (Frame enlargement by Gerhard Ullmann)

himself admits in his memoirs.[20] But these scenes are only too truthful from another perspective, that of the film's audience during World War II. The shelling of Kolberg in 1807 becomes the bombing of Hamburg, Berlin, and Dresden in the years between the first heavy air attacks on German cities and the apocalyptic spring of 1945.

At the end of this drawn-out depiction of exceptional carnage, the town, in the distance, is still smoking from French cannon fire; but in the foreground, a small tree is bringing forth fresh shoots. The argument of the sequence appears clear enough: bravery and fortitude in the face of danger, resisting the enemy even at terrible costs to oneself and one's family and community, will lead to salvation.

The promise of salvation held out by the defense of Kolberg consists of peace and reconstruction. But the film does not end here. The long flashback, which has shown Kolberg's suffering and survival, blends six years forward to the final part of the framing tale with which the film begins and ends and which now points to the lesson that the siege taught Prussia in 1813, and that through the audience's identification with its ancestors it is teaching the men and women of 1945. The lesson, of course, is that they must fight again, or continue to fight. Only then can the young tree really bloom. It should be added that new life is not the only promised outcome. A second, contradictory theme surfaces repeatedly in the words and actions of various characters: dying in war, whatever the outcome, is a blessing.

Although the film's argument seems straightforward, the images that carry it, and the aesthetic and psychological reactions they evoke in the audience, are more ambiguous. Why does the film emphasize and even exaggerate the killing of German soldiers and civilians and the destruction of Kolberg? And further, how would German audiences of the time react to this overemphasis? In effect, Goebbels raised both questions when he ordered Harlan in the fall of 1944 to delete long scenes of the fighting and shelling. He even answered the second one by telling Harlan: "The incessant killing and dying would irritate and disturb the viewer.

Kolberg comes under French cannon fire: a call to resist or a message of defeat? (Frame enlargement by Gerhard Ullmann)

Such scenes might be appropriate in a pacifistic film, but not for the 'heroic saga of Kolberg.' " Goebbels thought that the film "created a sense of resignation."[21]

Harlan might have responded to this criticism by stressing the sensationalism and appeal of the images and, further, by pointing out that the film had to show enough of the horrors of war to ensure that the audience would identify the French cannon of 1807 and the Allied bombers as two facets of the same destructive force directed against Germans. Only after recognizing the present in the past could the audience come to believe that Prussia's victory in the Wars of Liberation would be repeated in Germany's survival and triumph in 1945.

Nevertheless, Goebbels may have understood the subliminal reaction of the German viewer better than did Harlan. Perhaps he also had a clearer sense of unconscious tendencies in the filmmakers themselves and in the larger German society, tendencies that people still managed to suppress or that were held in check by the control mechanisms of the regime.

By the time *Kolberg* was shown, German audiences must have found it discouraging rather than bracing—and they might have found the film even more troubling had they seen the uncut version, with its still greater emphasis on carnage. How was it that the film had moved in this direction? The possibility that Harlan intended to send a subversive message can be excluded. After the war, he did not claim to have done so, and it was unlikely on other grounds as well. Although Harlan never joined the Nazi Party, he was not an opponent of the regime. He was an ambitious professional who accepted his environment as it was, avoided distasteful and dangerous situations, even helped a few victims, but in the end always gave in and went along.

It accords better with the evidence to see the film as expressing broad tendencies, whether or not they are consciously or fully understood by the individuals they influence. Of course, this raises the basic question of the extent to which an art form—even as collaborative an art form as film—serves as a conduit for general attitudes and emotions. But probably everyone would agree that the Propaganda Ministry and its filmmakers tried to be aware of the feelings of their audience, so that they could either reinforce these feelings or oppose them.

Goebbels is a special case. He knew all there was to know about the course the war was taking, but his ideological compulsions tended to insulate him from the central fact that Germany was being defeated, and at the same time made him sharply sensitive to other people's discouragement, readiness to compromise, and ideological slackness. With few exceptions, the men and women who worked for him shared neither his certainty nor his determination. Inevitably, they were influenced by the destruction all around them and by the fear of worse to come.

These pressures created a phenomenon in Germany that began to show itself not long after the war began and became pronounced in its last months. Symptoms of fatigue and a freezing of creativity appear not only in works of high culture, where they had been evident for years, but also increasingly in the popular media and in their application to politics in such forms as radio plays, films, posters, and cartoons. The National Socialist movement had not yet celebrated its thirtieth anniversary, but it was showing signs of old age. Considering the situation in which the Third Reich now found itself, discouragement and depression—even if still masked—were reasonable reactions. A case in point is *Der grosse König* (Germany, 1942), the last film celebrating Frederick the Great, the regime's favorite historical symbol for fighting to the end, which it has often been noted, depicts the king as a man prematurely aged by harsh experience, showing signs of resignation, even of melancholy.

Among other films and works in other media that contain similar hints, one appears especially pertinent to a discussion of *Kolberg*. As the Allied forces advanced into Germany at the beginning of 1945, preparations were made to defend the towns and cities in their path. Frankfurt, among others, was declared to be a "city in the front line." One of the means of mobilizing the population for the final struggle was a poster by the well-known German designer Hans Schweitzer, who signed his work with the pseudonym Mjölnir, the hammer with which the Norse god of war destroyed his enemies. Schweitzer had been a member of the Nazi Party since the 1920s, a collaborator of Goebbels in the propaganda war to win Berlin over to National Socialism. After 1933, he entered the Propaganda Ministry and was active in the campaign to rid Germany of expressionism and abstract art—he helped organized the exhibition of degenerate art in Munich—and to develop a new populist realism in tune with the values of the Third Reich. For these and other services, Schweitzer was rewarded with the title of professor and eventually with the honorary SS rank of brigadier general.[22] A man with his record could be expected to supply Frankfurt with a poster in the most uncompromising National Socialist tradition. The poster shows an elderly worker holding a swastika, a young woman—her right arm bandaged—and a boy in the uniform of

"Frankfurt, city in the frontline, will be held!" This poster's heroic message is not matched by its image of self-destruction and of physical and emotional weariness. A few changes would make it an appropriate poster for *Kolberg*.

an air force auxiliary all standing, ready to fight, on the rubble to which Allied bombers had reduced the city. This little group is surrounded by flames and by the legend "Frankfurt, city in the front line, will be held!"

It is not difficult to recognize similarities between the poster and the sequence of scenes in *Kolberg* that depict the shelling of the town, the fire, and the general destruction in which men and women do not suffer passively but continue to fight. Even the Frankfurt cathedral in the left background of the poster, symbol of the city and appealing to traditional religious values, which in times of crisis the regime was prepared to tolerate and exploit, has its counterpart in the film: the shelling of Kolberg is accompanied by the ringing of church bells and by an ethereal choir, a soundtrack that raises the images of violence and destruction to a transcendent struggle between good and evil. Like the film, the poster preaches obedience to a sacred cause, continued resistance, and determination to hold out to the end.

But if the poster's overt message is one of defiance, its image is one of despair. The three figures on the pile of rubble appear both grim and hopeless. They stand on the ruins of their physical world, while the confrontation of the cathedral with the pagan swastika has turned their spiritual world into a maze of ambiguities. Most startling, at the top of the poster, the flames almost blend with the red flag, which itself is split like a representation of fire. Is Schweitzer implying that the swastika and the regime for which it stands are responsible for the flames? However this is interpreted, the poster's heroic call to action is not supported by its image.

What is the designer expressing in this document of the Third Reich *in extremis?* Is it an admission of defeat? Does he hint at disillusionment of even the party faithful? A statement by Schweitzer at his denazification trial after the war may lend some credence to this reading. He now accused the regime in which he had believed—"only we were badly led."[23] Or should his poster be seen as a document of National Socialist nihilism?

The poster, which, incidentally, failed to rouse the inhabitants of Frankfurt to fight Patton's Third Army, is more open than *Kolberg* in giving signals of despair. But the film sends similar signals. On the surface, it calls for sacrifice for a great cause in phrases and symbols that after years of repetition had become drearily familiar to its audience. Beneath this layer of martial rhetoric, though, the film conveys two other meanings, which were unspoken but to which Germans had become strongly sensitized by 1945. One restates at length the basic nihilism of Hitler,

Goebbels, and their closest followers, which in the last months of the war broke completely into the open, to the point where destruction was ordered to punish the country for not having shown itself worthy of National Socialism, and for its own sake—in the final analysis, violence being the movement's only response to any problem or challenge. Responding to the nihilism of the leaders was a different message by their followers, which Goebbels clearly recognized when he criticized Harlan for making the shelling of the town too gruesome: weariness and the recognition of defeat.

That *Kolberg* is burdened with three contradictory messages is one reason for its raggedness and lack of balance. But in conveying these messages, the film accurately reflects the state of German public opinion in the last dreadful months of the war.

NOTES

1. The figure is accepted without question by most authors, although Rolf Aurich suggests a degree of skepticism when he writes that the number of men and the amounts of material used in the film are the stuff of legend. See his "Film als Durchhalteration: Kolberg von Veit Harlan" in *Das Ufa-Buch,* ed. Hans-Michael Bock and Michael Tötenberg (Frankfurt: Zweitausendeins, 1992), p. 462. Certainly not one-tenth of the 187,000 soldiers that Veit Harlan claims actually do appear in the film's battle and crowd scenes, and even with the episodes that were cut on Goebbels's insistence, the percentage would not have appreciably increased. Since the film was shot over fourteen months, with many interruptions and retakes, soldiers would have worked only for a few days at a time, their place being taken by others when the next mass scene was filmed. For example, there are the 4,000 sailors Harlan mentions. They interrupted a training course to serve as extras in the scene of French soldiers trying to advance over ground flooded by the defenders. The scene was probably shot in a few days. But Harlan speaks vaguely of the sailors "having to hang around for months" (*Im Schatten meiner Filme,* ed. H. C. Opfermann [Gütersloh: Sigbert Mohn, 1966], pp. 187–88).

2. Harlan, *Im Schatten meiner Filme,* p. 189. That even major figures in the production are not necessarily the most reliable witnesses is also indicated by Kristina Söderbaum, Harlan's wife and the female lead in *Kolberg,* who includes an inaccurate outline of the film's plot in her memoirs, *Nichts bleibt immer so,* 2d ed. (Munich: Herbig, 1992), p. 305.

3. Aurich, "Film als Durchhalteration," p. 462.

4. David Welch, *Propaganda and the German Cinema, 1933–1945* (New York: Oxford University Press, 1983), p. 225. The statement is repeated in different words on page 232. Oddly, in view of his very detailed outline of the plot, Welch writes that in the film, "Napoleon, alarmed at the losses he has sustained, orders his cavalry to pull back." This scene is missing in the prints of the film I have seen and seems unlikely, since Napoleon is not present at the siege.

5. It suggests the relative strategic insignificance of the siege—as opposed to its political and psychological implications for subsequent events in Prussia—that the map volume used at West Point, Vincent J. Esposito and John Elting, eds., *A Military History and Atlas of the Napoleonic Wars* (New York: Praeger, 1964), merely indicates on its general map of the 1807 campaign that the town was held by Prussian forces, but does not mention the siege in its text.

6. Welch, *Propaganda and the German Cinema*, p. 226.

7. Ibid., p. 234.

8. Quoted in Gerhard Schoenberner, "Kolberg," in *Kolberg, Ufa Magazin Nr. 20* (Berlin: Deutsches Historisches Museum, 1992), p. 3, part of the catalogue for the exhibition *Die UFA—Das deutsche Bilderimperium* (Berlin: Deutsches Historisches Museum, 1992).

9. Welch, *Propaganda and the German Cinema*, p. 229, n. 98.

10. Ibid., p. 226.

11. Harlan, *Im Schatten meiner Filme*, p. 182.

12. Richard Taylor, *Film Propaganda, Soviet Russia and Nazi Germany* (London: Croom Helm, 1979), p. 218.

13. Harlan, *Im Schatten meiner Filme*, p. 182. It might be added that in the film's battle scenes, un-uniformed or partly uniformed militia—the *Volkssturm*—are scarcely in evidence. Indeed, civilians in uniform, which some commentators regard as a major theme of the film, are central to only one scene: they drill in the town square before the siege begins and arouse the ridicule of the regular army officer commanding the garrison. The film does not appeal to civilians to take up arms, but demands that they support the armed forces materially and psychologically, and accept the most severe losses without complaint, let alone defeatism. That, incidentally, comes closer to the reality of 1813 than does the legend of a people in arms. In the spring and autumn campaign of that year, which drove the French out of Germany, plans were drafted for the *Landsturm*—as it was called then—but it did not take part in the fighting.

14. Quoted in Taylor, *Film Propaganda*, p. 216.

15. Joseph Goebbels to Veit Harlan, June 1, 1943, in Harlan, *Im Schatten meiner Filme*, p. 183.

16. Goebbels, speech, February 18, 1943, in *Goebbels Reden, 1939–1945*, ed. Helmut Heiber (Düsseldorf: Droste, 1972), p. 208.

17. The opening chant actually combines two poems. The first lines, a celebration of death for the fatherland, come from Theodor Körner's "Brotherhood Song Before Battle." The defiant proclamation "The people rise, The storm erupts" is the opening of Körner's poem "Men and Rogues," which contrasts courage and cowardice. In Körner's original German, the words are less an appeal to the people to rise than an assertion that the people are rising.

18. Nettelbeck, not Gneisenau or Maria's lover, is the film's leading figure. The character's stature is also reflected in a poster advertising the film, which gives precedence to Heinrich George as Nettelbeck and Kristina Söderbaum as Maria.

19. Harlan, *Im Schatten meiner Filme*, p. 189.

20. Ibid., p. 184.

21. Ibid., p. 184.

22. On Hans Schweitzer, see Peter Paret, "God's Hammer," *Proceedings of the American Philosophical Society* 139 (1992): 226–46, which analyzes Schweitzer's posters and political cartoons, and traces his career on the basis of such contemporary sources as Goebbels's diaries and the records of Schweitzer's denazification trial and appeals. At his trial and the appeal hearings, Schweitzer (much like Harlan, but with far less justification) succeeded in passing himself off as a harmless if politically naive artist. Schweitzer's indictment did not mention his posters, or his membership in the commission that cleansed German museums of art regarded as un-German, or the equally shameful fact that, as Goebbels's agent, he hounded one of Germany's greatest artists, the sculptor and dramatist Ernst Barlach, in the last years of his life by closing a small exhibition in which Barlach was represented and threatening to prohibit him from working as a sculptor. Schweitzer's trial and appeals resulted in a slap on the wrist, and after some years he found employment in an agency of the Federal Republic of Germany.

23. Quoted in Paret, "God's Hammer," p. 244.

4

Kolberg (Germany, 1945): The Goebbels Diaries and Poland's Kołobrzeg Today

DAVID CULBERT

We shall not flag or fail. We shall go on to the end, we shall fight in France, we shall fight on the seas and oceans, we shall fight with growing confidence and growing strength in the air, we shall defend our island, whatever the cost may be, we shall fight on the beaches, we shall fight on the landing grounds, we shall fight in the fields and in the streets, we shall fight in the hills; we shall never surrender, and even if, which I do not for a moment believe, this island or a large part of it were subjugated and starving, then our Empire beyond the seas, armed and guarded by the British fleet, would carry on the struggle until, in God's good time, the new world, with all its power and might, steps forth to the rescue and the liberation of the old. (Winston Churchill, June 4, 1940)

You weren't born in Kolberg, Gneisenau. You were ordered to Kolberg, but we—we grew up here. We know every stone, every corner, every house. We won't surrender even if we have to claw the ground with our nails. In Kolberg we don't give up. They'll have to cut off our hands or slay us one by one. Gneisenau, you can't humiliate this old man by surrendering our town to Napoleon. I promised our King that we'd rather be buried under our rubble than capitulate. Gneisenau, Gneisenau . . . I've never begged anyone, but now I will get down on my knees. Kolberg must not surrender, Gneisenau. (Nettelbeck to Gneisenau, *Kolberg* script)

The story of the defeat of Napoleon and his army in Russia, in fact, is a tale which I myself heard in many versions while growing up in Elbing, about 125 miles east of Kolberg. It was told to me by my mother, who had herself grown up hearing eyewitness reports from her own grandmother, who had been a young girl in 1807. The moral was that even the strongest and most confident can be defeated by courageous resistance. (Hans J. Fabian, 1994)

With the important exception of Peter Paret, most historians who write about *Kolberg* (Germany, 1945) belittle the film. They note the wasteful use of thousands of soldiers as extras, when Germany needed every available man for front-line duty. They note the enormous expense of this Agfacolor picture, at a time when money was desperately needed for war munitions. They question the logic of waiting until the anniversary of Hitler's coming to power, January 30, 1945, to release a film into a Germany with fewer and fewer movie theaters not bombed out, at a moment when everyone knew the war was long-since lost.

Jay Baird, in his fine book *To Die for Germany: Heroes in the Nazi Pantheon*, suggests that the purpose of *Kolberg* is simply Goebbels's cinematic justification for a hero's death, and he quotes the statement of Gneisenau to Nettelbeck to make his point: "Now we can die together." Erwin Leiser analyzes *Kolberg* at length in his final chapter of *Nazi Cinema*, entitled "Götterdämmerung." He underscores the futility of the film, and the impossibility of its message finding an audience capable of being persuaded by a call for resistance unto death.[1]

None of these attempts to dismiss the presumptive overt propaganda content of the film are incorrect. In January 1945, no motion picture, however brilliant, could prevent imminent defeat. But it is instructive to look again at the dramaturgy of *Kolberg* and to ask to what degree the characters have believable lines or make important points—in short, to what degree the film demonstrates the expertise of many of Germany's finest actors and actresses.

Most who see *Kolberg* agree that the best performance is given by Heinrich George, born not too far from Kolberg at Stettin in 1893, and destined to die in Russian captivity at the Sachsenhausen concentration camp in September 1946.[2] George's superb performance in the rarely seen *Kolberg* is far superior to his excellent portrayal of the father in *Hitlerjunge Quex* (Germany, 1933). His preeminence as an actor on stage and in film led to a special fiftieth-birthday celebration in Berlin's Renaissance Theater on October 9, 1943; Goebbels brought his own, as well as Hitler's, personal best wishes. George was extremely corpulent. His earnestness might not be to everyone's taste, but he conveys a palpable sense of authority, as in *Kolberg,* where he plays the historic figure of a brewmaster and is made to resemble Paul von Hindenburg, Germany's national hero from World War I. George knew this story well many years before Veit Harlan's film went into production. In July 1932, he had played the title role in *Nettelbeck*, a play by the now-forgotten Heinrich Römer. The location: the outdoor summer theater in Kolberg. In a surviving letter, George writes that he is spending his summer holiday in Kolberg.[3]

The argument of the film—that the idea of a people's army is powerfully contested by tradition-bound military officers—is given tremendous interest by the brilliance of Paul Wegener, one of Germany's greatest actors, whose career is virtually synonymous with the history of German feature-film production. By 1944, Wegener had long-since turned to directing as well and understood that he had the task of making persuasive the ideas the film sought to condemn. Anyone interested in how to present a tough, hide-bound military commander, stubbornly convinced of the correctness of his methods, will do well to study Wegener's Loucadou, truly a virtuoso performance. Colonel Loucadou, of course, loses to Gneisenau, but not before putting up a powerful resistance.

Not one of the other male roles is poorly acted, though not every character is effectively delineated. Gustav Diessl, the romantic lead with Leni Riefenstahl in *Sturm über Montblanc* (Germany, 1930), plays the one-dimensional heroism of Lieutenant Ferdinand von Schill in an appropriate manner.[4] Horst Casper, one of Germany's most successful actors, does what he can with the part of Gneisenau, also a rather one-dimensional role, difficult to bring off because one must forever be earnest, handsome, manly, and the wave of the future when it comes to recognizing the value of a citizen army. Claus Clausen has little to do as Friedrich Wilhelm III; farmer Werner gets everything his part can hope for as portrayed by Otto Wernicke, who specialized in such older man-of-the-people roles. Kurt Meisel does a very effective job as Claus, farmer Werner's son, ruined by too much time in Strasbourg learning French cosmopolitan ways, including, in particular, the lesson that pride in one's own town is the mark of a country bumpkin. Claus is a defeatist, and his role tells a good bit as to which persons were considered likely fifth-columnists in Germany as the war neared its end.[5]

Neither woman's role is well done. Irene von Meyendorff plays the part of Queen Luise as it is written, and the result is utterly impossible to believe. Kristina Söderbaum, Harlan's beautiful Swedish wife, is lifeless in her thankless role as Maria. The work's greatest dramaturgical weakness is the failure of each romantic interlude to persuade viewers that they should possibly care about what happens to Maria. *Kolberg* is a film by men, about men, and about war and the doctrines of war. Women just do not matter.

Harlan has surely exaggerated the number of extras employed in the film, and he seems to deploy a hundred times as many cannon for Napoleon to use as was the case in 1807, but the war scenes are persuasive. Moreover, the cannon assault on Kolberg is visually effective. It is interesting to see how respectful *Kolberg* is to the historic figure of Napoleon, presented as more of a military genius than Germany's enemy.

The Goebbels diary fragments returned from Moscow in 1992. As edited by Elke Frölich of the Institut für Zeitgeschichte, the entries reveal the original purpose Goebbels had in mind for the film, and how much debate over the film's dramaturgy delayed completion of the project.

> *May 7, 1943: With Veit Harlan and Wolfgang Liebeneiner.* I discuss Harlan's next assignment: *Kolberg.* In this film Harlan will depict an example of manly courage and a civilian populace's strength to resist when facing a desperate situation. This film will above all offer a powerful lesson in areas subject to air raids. The film will be based entirely on historical facts. Harlan who at first tried to avoid taking on this assignment since he wanted to make a film about Beethoven, is now red hot for the assignment *[ganz Feuer und Flamme].* In eight days he has produced a splendid outline and intends to start shooting by the end of June. He promised the film's premiere for Christmas. By then we shall probably be able to put it to good use.

> *May 25, 1943:* [Dr. Werner] Naumann reports that he has been successful in locating the necessary contingents for implementing the Kolberg film. I am hoping for extraordinarily much from this Harlan film. It fits exactly the military and political landscape that we shall probably have to record by the time this film is shown.

> [*June 1, 1943:* Harlan signs contract with Goebbels.]

> *June 5, 1943:* I read until late at night the Harlan treatment for the new Kolberg film. Harlan has unfortunately, as is often the case with him, made a Söderbaum film out of a Nettelbeck film. Instead of Nettelbeck, a young girl named Maria is central to the entire action, and his wife Söderbaum is of course intended for this part. It will take a great deal of effort to make Harlan give up the idea in his treatment. Nevertheless it must be done since I put such great hope for our inner peace of mind in this Kolberg film, in which so much money is invested. Who knows in what position we will find ourselves. We must therefore have a film ready to encourage and support the toughness of civilian resistance. In such matters women have less of a say than men. I predict that the Kolberg film, if properly done as I envision, will do us great service in the coming winter.

June 6, 1943: Harlan's new Kolberg treatment, which I have now read through, does not fulfill my expectations. He has unfortunately produced more of a Söderbaum than a Nettelbeck film.

June 14, 1943: In the evening a few persons come for a visit. I talk to Harlan about his Kolberg treatment. It must have a nationalistic concept. As things stand, it has too simple a patriotic structure. Also Nettelbeck must occupy a more central part. Harlan has structured the treatment a bit too broadly. The danger exists that the result will be too long, exactly as was the case with the Frederick the Great film. To avoid this outcome something must be done.

July 14, 1943: I talk at midday to the German film producers and directors. . . . I must find a bit of rest for myself. I am, thanks to the tensions of the recent weeks, under heavy stress and overworked. I take this opportunity to read the reworked Harlan treatment for the Kolberg film. It is now enormously improved over the first draft. I believe that work on the film can now begin. It will surely be a monumental achievement of German film art.

July 15, 1943: I have a detailed discussion about the Kolberg film with those responsible. Harlan pays too much attention to the disaster scenes and misses the more intimate moments. He must cut down a bit on his monumental plans and shape a film a bit more in the style of *Mrs. Miniver* [U.S. 1942]. It will be difficult to make this clear to him, but there is nothing for it but once again to revise the script.[6]

Shooting began on October 27, 1943; some scenes were reshot as late as July 17, 1944. A rough cut was finally ready for screening on November 30.

December 1, 1944: In the evening *Kolberg,* the new Harlan color film is shown. It is a true masterpiece of the director's art. Harlan has positioned it so skilfully, that one would pretty much suspect that it was first put into production just three weeks ago; it offers an answer to all the questions that currently preoccupy the German people. I predict an extraordinary success for this film. We will have to make a number of cuts and changes, since Harlan in various places repeats his familiar mistakes, including mystical chorus parts and superfluous on-screen portrayals. I will have this approved for public distribution as quickly as possible. This film has the same meaning for the mood of the German people today as a battlefield victory.

December 2, 1944: Cultural life, as ever, is of intense interest to him [Hitler]. I told him about the new Kolberg film, and described for him a few of the scenes, which moved the *Führer* almost to the point of tears. He asked me to release the film as quickly as possible, and described it after my summary as a successful battle in the political leadership of the war. . . . It is already daylight when I say goodbye to the *Führer.*[7]

December 3, 1944: I screen *Kolberg,* the new Harlan color film, a second time. I again conclude that this is a first-rate political masterpiece, which needs but a few slight editing changes; then this film, as the *Führer* noted correctly [last night], will function as a successful battle in the political leadership of the sixth year of war.

The slight changes needed yet further discussion. Goebbels met with Veit Harlan, the director, and Hans Hinkel, *Reichsfilmintendant.* On December 7, 1944, in Goebbels's private screening room in his home on Göringstrasse, "about 150 Nazi leaders" screened the rough cut. Their comments led to yet more changes.

December 12, 1944: I speak with Professor Harlan about the necessary cuts in the Kolberg film, ones that will be very easy to make. It takes a great deal of effort to discourage him from pursuing his idea for his latest film, *The Merchant of Venice,* using the actual verses. It is impossible to use Shakespeare's exact words in a film that will be two hours long. It is ridiculous and absurd and will at best end up as nothing but a literary experiment. Such experiments are impossible now, when we can make at best only 42 films per year.

December 23, 1944: In the evening the final Harlan version of the new Kolberg film is screened, to which I have invited Professor Liebeneiner and Heinrich George as well. Instead of improving the film, Harlan has made it worse. He coarsened the scenes of chaos and destruction in the city, so that I fear the major part of the viewing public will refuse to see the film, given the current situation. It must be radically re-cut to make it ready for release. I hope in spite of this that it will be done by the time of its premiere on January 30. I decide the time is right to discuss with Professor Liebeneiner a variety of specific film matters; he has taken over the direction of the Ufa slowly and with evident success. George is as ever the courageous old fighter *[alte tapfere Kämpfer]* for our concerns, who sticks with us for good or ill *[auf Gedeih und Verderb].* . . . I will take so little notice of Christmas as possible.

In the end, Goebbels and Hinkel asked Harlan's colleague, director Wolfgang Liebeneiner, to make the final cuts, which he did by January 3, 1945.[8]

Let us take another look at *Kolberg*'s message of "never surrender," remembering that Goebbels actually revised the major propaganda speeches in the film, increasing the historical significance of the words spoken by some of the principal actors. In the film, the speech calling for last-ditch resistance is made by Nettelbeck, on his knees as he begs Gneisenau not to give up the fight (Gneisenau, as Peter Paret reminds us, is actually only testing Nettelbeck's resolve). Is what Nettelbeck says totally unpersuasive? Heinrich George grew up near Kolberg; he knew that the war was going badly for Germany when the film was being shot. Why not presume that as a professional actor, he would indeed put his heart into making the case for love of one's own country? Is this really so different from Churchill's brilliant calculation when he delivered his speech to the House of Commons in June 1940? True, Churchill began by reminding his listeners that "wars are not won by evacuations." He admitted that Dunkirk was a "colossal military disaster," as indeed it was. But what is the literal difference between Churchill's "we shall never surrender" and Nettelbeck's "Kolberg must not surrender"? The phrases are virtually identical, which is not to ignore for a moment the enormous difference in context. Still, it is important to ensure that the test for speeches urging last-ditch sacrifice on a civilian populace not be simply a moral judgment as to the worthiness of the speaker or government in question.

There is one other significant connection between the contents of the film and its relation to Goebbel's own thinking—the use of the line from Theodor Körner's poem "Männer und Buben": "Das Volk steht auf, der Sturm bricht los!" (The people rise, the storm erupts), with which Goebbels ended his "Total War" speech at Berlin's *Sportpalast* on February 18, 1943. Goebbels changed Körner's text slightly, nevertheless intending that his most important wartime speech recall an earlier era to instill resolve in his listeners. It is not mere coincidence that this line also appears in *Kolberg* at the end of the film, spoken by Gneisenau as he reflects on the possibility of a people's army assisting regular troops against supposedly hopeless odds.

Reality proved indeed that the odds were hopeless. The city of Kolberg was nearly 80 percent destroyed in 1945. Peter Paret reminds us that

> one needs to be careful not to misinterpret the motives of the German defenders. Of course Goebbels tried to stimulate the defense with references to 1807, but that was not the reason for defending the town. Kolberg was filled with refugees, most of them from Lower Pomerania *[Hinterpommern]* who were trying to escape to the West. The town and the port were held until naval vessels had evacuated the civilians, then the remaining force of 2000 soldiers left the empty town—to Goebbels' disgust. It would be wrong to give Goebbels credit for the defense.[9]

True, but the final entries of the Goebbels diaries, all translated into idiomatic English in Hugh Trevor-Roper's edition, make clear the enormous psychological importance Goebbels placed on Kolberg's not surrendering to Soviet troops:

February 28, 1945: Bolshevists to Neustettin–Kolberg railway.

March 4, 1945: Soviet tanks are already outside Kolberg. Our position in Pomerania may be said to have disintegrated totally.

March 5, 1945: Kolberg is surrounded. . . . The Military Commandant of Kolberg—if he can be called so—made a proposition to the *Führer* that the town be surrendered without a fight. The *Führer* immediately removed him and put a younger officer in his place. Have these degenerate generals no sense of history or of responsibility? Does a present-day Military Commandant of Kolberg nurture the ambition to emulate a Loucadou rather than a Gneisenau?

March 10, 1945: Heavy attacks on Kolberg repulsed with heavy losses to garrison.

March 13, 1945: Attacks on Kolberg were repulsed.

March 16, 1945: The enemy has forced his way into Kolberg and fierce street fighting has flared up. By the day before yesterday a total of 40,000 out of the 50,000 refugees assembled in Kolberg had been evacuated. . . . In Kolberg the final battles are apparently taking place.

March 18, 1945: We have now had to evacuate Kolberg. The town, which has been defended with such extraordinary heroism, could no longer be held. I will ensure that the evacuation of Kolberg is not mentioned in the OKW [*Ober Kommando der Wehrmacht* (Military High Command)] report. In view of the severe psychological repercussions on the Kolberg film we could do without that for the moment.

March 20, 1945: Kolberg too fell into enemy hands.

April 17, 1945: [Goebbels summoned his Propaganda Ministry staff, some fifty men, to meet with him in Berlin. He spoke of his admiration for the film *Kolberg* and discussed the possibility of making an even more splendid color feature film.]

April 24, 1945: [Soviet troops occupy Berlin-Babelsberg.][10]

In his diary, Goebbels connects the siege of Kolberg in 1945 with the siege of 1807, and he follows the battle of 1945 by referring to the film's depiction of Loucadou and Gneisenau. Is this not an unusual purpose for a policy of civilian sacrifice? A town must not surrender to the enemy, no matter what the cost, because it will undermine the propaganda message of a recently released feature film. It is hard to see why the military commander of Kolberg had to be replaced in March 1945 by a "younger officer," unless Goebbels could not bear the thought of surrender when his new film showed that victory could be achieved against hopeless odds. Dying to maintain the integrity of a feature film's propaganda message is an unusual definition of patriotism. It must certainly have seemed bizarre in nearby Königsberg to watch *Kolberg* in those theaters not bombed out, and then help defend the city as a member of the *Volkssturm*.

The film needs as well to be placed in a different sort of filmic context— its connection as half of a two-part propaganda exercise to encourage civilian resistance to air raids, the other being the uncompleted lavish feature *Das Leben geht weiter* (Life Goes On), which Goebbels intended as a companion to *Kolberg*, this time a film set in Berlin in 1943/1944. Liebeneiner directed this film; Heinrich George, in his last appearance before the camera, played the small part of an airplane manufacturer with a new "miracle" product. Scenes were shot near Lüneburg on April 14, 1945, literally one day before the area fell to the British. *Das Leben geht weiter* is more consciously based on the tone and style of William Wyler's *Mrs. Miniver* (U.S., 1942), a sentimental tale of English women persevering in wartime, a favorite film of both Franklin D. Roosevelt and Joseph Goebbels. Goebbels had access to a print in Berlin that he screened a number of times. He wanted to give Liebeneiner the idea of the sort of sincere propaganda he envisioned. To show him how German perseverance should be portrayed, he invited Liebeneiner to join him for an October 13, 1944, screening.[11]

The entries for 1943 of the Goebbels diary help explain the lengthy gestation of *Kolberg,* whose original release date was to have been Christmas 1943, a filmic answer to German civilian fears following massive air raids over Hamburg and Berlin. Goebbels really did take a personal interest in the dramaturgy of the film. He intended *Kolberg* to turn Nettelbeck into a hero, even if this meant time-consuming revisions of the script, each of which Goebbels read carefully.

In the end, artistic demands took precedence over practical considerations in the completion of a propaganda film with Germany's most lavish production values. Goebbels was more concerned that the dramaturgy of *Kolberg* be right than it find civilian release in time to make sense as a propaganda vehicle, an ironic comment about the practicality of one who considered himself a consummate propagandist.

NOTES

1. Jay W. Baird, *To Die for Germany: Heroes in the Nazi Pantheon* (Bloomington: Indiana University Press, 1990), pp. 241–42; Erwin Leiser, *Nazi Cinema,* trans. Gertrud Mander and David Wilson (London: Secker & Warburg, 1974), pp. 121–33. For a similar interpretation, see Friedrich P. Kahlenberg, "Preussen als Filmsujet in der propagandasprache der NS-Zeit," in *Preussen im Film,* ed. Axel Marquardt and Heinz

Rathsack (Reinbek bei Hamburg: Rowohlt, 1981), pp. 161–64. For an effective overview of the production of *Kolberg,* see *Kolberg, Ufa Magazin Nr. 20* (Berlin: Deutsches Historisches Museum, 1992). See also Rolf Aurich, "Film als Durchhalteration: Kolberg von Veit Harlan," in *Das Ufa-Buch,* ed. Hans-Michael Bock and Michael Töteberg (Frankfurt: Zweitausandeins, 1992), pp. 462–65. The script for *Kolberg,* in my English translation, is found as a microfiche supplement to the *Historical Journal of Film, Radio and Television* 14, no. 4 (1994).

2. Heinrich George was arrested and released twice in the spring of 1945; denounced for a third time, he was arrested on June 22 and taken to Alexanderplatz by Soviet soldiers and, at the beginning of 1946, to Sachsenhausen. He died of a ruptured appendix, though the official Soviet report claimed bronchial pneumonia. George's son, using reports from forensic experts who disinterred his father's remains—he showed me color photographs of the skeletal figure—had his father interred again on October 16, 1994, in Zehlendorf, in a Berlin cemetary a few minutes from the family home. Interview with Jan George, April 21, 1995, Berlin.

3. Peter Laregh, *Heinrich George: Komödiant seiner Zeit* (Munich: Langen Müller, 1992), pp. 172, 231, 233; the performance is listed on p. 334. The letter is part of the Heinrich George Papers, currently in the possession of Jan George. I am grateful to Jan George for permission to use this archive. Another letter in the archive indicates that *Kolberg* was a historical parallel that appealed to those seeking comfort in the 1930s by remembering the hard times of an earlier day. Carl Echtermeier wrote to George on June 28, 1933, including a film treatment for *Kapitän Nettelbeck,* "a national film from Prussia's darkest days." In 1935, Lloydfilm announced production of a film about Kolberg, which also came to naught. See *Film-Kurier,* March 6, 1935, cited in Klaus Kanzog, *"Staatspolitisch besonders wertvoll": Ein Handbuch zu 30 deutschen Spielfilmen der Jahre 1934 bis 1945* (Munich: Diskurs Film, 1994), p. 356. I am grateful to Michael Schaudig, the publisher, for getting this book to me by express mail.

4. "The figure of Schill and the fate of his officers and men has long been a part of the Prussian-German myth of the Napoleonic-era struggle for independence and unity. It is therefore not surprising that the fate of Schill's officers at the hands of the French had already been the subject of two earlier German feature films. *Die elf Schill'schen Offiziere* (Germany, 1926), was directed by Rudolf Meinert; it was the fifth most successful box office success in Germany 1926–27. Meinert directed and also wrote the script for a 1932 sound version of the same film, in which Veit Harlan played the part of one of the eleven officers" (Hans J. Fabian, *"Kolberg:* A Comment and Personal Note," *Historical Journal of Film, Radio and Television* 14, no. 4 [1994]: 455).

5. "Claus is a Frenchified, violin-playing weakling. His demeanor, his mannerisms and his character bear an unmistakable resemblance to Peter Lorre's portrayal of the obsequious child-molester/murderer in Fritz Lang's *M* (Germany, 1931). Klaus's voice, and even some of the lines scripted for him are pure Lorre, and as such are obviously meant to help the audience associate Klaus with a character the Nazis attacked as indicative of Weimar depravity" (ibid., p. 454).

6. *Die Tagebücher von Joseph Goebbels, Part II,* ed. Elke Fröhlich (Munich: Saur, 1993–1996). I am grateful to Klaus Saur for sending me volume 14 (October–December 1944) in time to include the December entries in this essay.

7. Part of the entry for December 2 is also found in *Joseph Goebbels Tagebücher, 1924–1945,* ed. Ralf Georg Reuth (Munich: Piper, 1992), vol. 5, p. 2112.

8. Haus-Christoph Blumenberg, *Das Leben geht weiter: Der letzte Film des Dritten Reichs* (Berlin: Rowohlt, 1993), p. 174. The *five* specific changes Goebbels ordered in the rough cut, including cutting some of the most horrifying battle scenes, are found in Kanzog, *"Staatspolitisch besonders wertvoll,"* pp. 357n.181, 361n.182. Kanzog provides a full list of credits and a guide to the reception of *Kolberg* in Germany *since* 1945.

9. Letter, Peter Paret to David Culbert, April 19, 1994.

10. *Final Entries, 1945: The Diaries of Joseph Goebbels,* ed. Hugh Trevor-Roper (New York: Putnam, 1978), pp. xxxi–xxxii. For the scholarly value of the Goebbels diaries, see David Culbert, "Leni Riefenstahl and the Diaries of Joseph Goebbels," *Historical Journal of Film, Radio and Television* 13, no. 1 (1993): 85–93.

11. See Blumenberg, *Das Leben geht weiter,* p. 118; in English, see Lee Marshall, "The Last Nazi Film," *Sunday Telegraph,* February 26, 1995, sec. 5, p. 1. *Mrs. Miniver,* to the disgust of the anonymous reviewer in *Documentary News Letter,* was an emotional success with English audiences as well: "You can sit at the Empire and hear practically the whole house weeping—a British audience with 3 years of war behind it crying at one of the phoniest war films that has ever been made" (quoted in Jeffrey Richards and Dorothy Sheridan, eds., *Mass-Observation at the Movies* [London: Routledge, 1987], p. 15).

Photo Essay: Kołobrzeg, Poland, 1994

PHOTOGRAPHS BY HANS-JOACHIM GROHMANN

TEXT BY DAVID CULBERT

In March 1994, Hans-Joachim Grohmann and I visited Kołobrzeg to photograph a city of 100,000 almost entirely destroyed in 1945. Kolberg, today again important as a health resort on the Baltic, suffered greatly after 1945 from the ideology and economic policies of the Polish Communists, who were happy to leave Kolberg's center largely in ruins. The Communists hoped to destroy history and religion, erecting monuments to only Soviet and Polish Communist heroes who had defeated the Nazis at Kolberg. One sees in the images on these pages a conscious effort to obliterate the design of the town's historic German center: an apartment house almost totally obscures the church's spire; an aluminum shopping center spoils the plaza in front of the church. An inexpensive aluminum bar is erected next to the historic Rathaus, the latter not just a town hall but the German word for "town hall."

Since 1987, and particularly since 1989, it has again been possible to add religious iconography to the World War II monuments. A wooden cross now marks the place where thousands of Poles died in the 1945 battle to free Kolberg. A plaque commemorates the visit of Pope John Paul II, a Pole, to Kolberg's Roman Catholic church. Even the extremes of Stalinist iconography have been removed from resistance memorials.

The town center is slowly being rebuilt to suggest how part of the town might have appeared in Hanseatic times. Gentrification of the downtown area is also under way. Indeed, today's Kołobrzeg is tourist-friendly; the restored Roman Catholic church is a place to worship and also a place for

Kolberg and the changing German–Polish border. Before 1919, and from 1939 to 1945, Kolberg, Danzig, and Königsberg were German. Today—renamed—Kołobrzeg and Gdansk are Polish. Königsberg, renamed Kalingrad, is in Russia. Poland's changing boundaries are a testament to its position between two powerful neighbors. The current Polish–German border is indicated by dashes; the relevant post-1945 boundary changes with Russia are marked by crosses. (Map by Bryon Weathers and Andrea Caillouet, Division of Instructional Support and Development, Louisiana State University, 1995. Reprinted by permission)

tourists to visit. The town center, however, will be a monument to its former Communist city planners as long as the shopping center in front of the church remains, and as long as the enormous apartment house obscures the church's spire. Something of Kolberg's German past can be seen only by removing the excesses of Poland's Communist past. Whose history is being remembered will continue to be the subject of continuing debate in Kolberg—or Kołobrzeg—for the forseeable future.

Left. On the beach at Kołobrzeg in 1994 stands a monument to victims of Hitler's fascism. Only recently was it possible to place a wooden cross at the base. (Photo by Hans-Joachim Grohmann. Reprinted by permission)

Below. Almost none of Hanseatic-era Kolberg survives, save this building, the tourist bureau. (Photo by Hans-Joachim Grohmann. Reprinted by permission)

Above. The Rathaus, where in the film Nettelbeck debates the future of the city with the town councillors, is directly across from the church. (Photo by Hans-Joachim Grohmann. Reprinted by permission)

Left. The massive façade of the church, constructed as a haven in time of military attack. An aluminum shopping center, built in the 1960s, is directly in front of the entrance to the church. (Photo by Hans-Joachim Grohmann. Reprinted by permission)

The reconstruction of historic Kolberg after forty years. The destruction of Kolberg in the film was done on sets at the Ufa studios in Berlin-Babelsberg, based on photographs from Kolberg, including this precise view of the church (see photograph on p. 59). "Big Star," the name on the sign on the right, is a Polish brand of "American" blue jeans. (Photo by Hans-Joachim Grohmann. Reprinted by permission)

5

Ivan's Childhood (USSR, 1962) and *Come and See* (USSR, 1985): Post-Stalinist Cinema and the Myth of World War II

DENISE J. YOUNGBLOOD

World War II, known in the former Soviet Union as the Great Fatherland War or Great Patriotic War, could have been invented as a subject for socialist realist cinema. With perhaps 20 to 27 million dead (a figure representing approximately 15 percent of the population) and Belorussia, Ukraine, and European Russia in smoldering ruins, it is difficult for anyone to exaggerate the space of the tragedy, the scope of the disaster, the scale of heroism. The Soviet government tried, however—and succeeded for a more than a generation.

The story of the victory against all odds lived on in countless museums and monuments dotting Russia and the other Soviet republics, particularly the European ones. It also survived in rites of memory (especially those connected with Victory Day, May 9) and the pilgrimages of schoolchildren and newlyweds to the shrines, cemeteries, and battlefields. The longevity of the myth of the Great Patriotic War, central to Soviet history in the second half of this century, never fails to startle the uninitiated.[1] It has, after all, been fifty years since war's end. Although other nations have their own myths (the "Good War" for Americans, yet another national humiliation for the Poles), no other combatant made the terrible sacrifices of the war into "Virtue" to nearly the extent as did the Soviets. By the Brezhnev era, the war cult had become a cornerstone of the old regime, and so the loss of faith in manufactured memory had significant political consequences.

Nowhere is this process of mythmaking and unmaking more concisely and vividly illustrated than in cinema. The history of the Soviet World War

II film, the subject of this chapter, is an important (indeed, essential) key to understanding the myth. Furthermore, the rise and self-destruction of the genre provides a paradigm for illustrating the disaffection of the postwar generation of film directors with the old order and the extent to which they were able to express that disaffection in late Soviet society. These issues will be explored in the following pages, first by sketching the genre's evolution from its inception in the war to the end of the Brezhnev era and then by examining in closer detail two seminal films: Andrei Tarkovskii's *Ivan's Childhood* (USSR, 1962) and Elem Klimov's *Come and See* (USSR, 1985).

Stalin's sophisticated propaganda machine was immediately ready to support the war effort, accustomed as it was to the twists and turns of Soviet domestic and foreign policy. During the war itself, the *entirety* of Soviet film production, both fiction and newsreel, focused on the war effort.[2]

Initially, films were predictable tales of heroic resistance tailored to the particular calamity of the war experience in the Soviet Union. They were surprisingly realistic in the sense that partisans, rather than the regular army, loomed large with women rather than men serving as protagonists, reflecting the harsh facts of war and the enormous loss of male lives at the front in the first six months of conflict. The classic example of this kind of war propaganda is Fridrikh Ermler's *She Defends Her Motherland* (USSR, 1943), the most famous of the "heroine" films. Although he is little known in the West, Ermler was an important director in the Soviet period. In *Motherland,* the beloved Soviet film star Vera Maretskaia plays a woman determined to avenge the deaths of her husband and child by becoming an uncompromisingly ruthless partisan leader—no gentle stay-at-home widows here.[3]

It is only at war's end, when victory was assured (along with his place in history—or so he thought), that Stalin supplanted these larger-than-life heroines and assumed center stage himself. The prime example is, of course, Mikhail Chiaureli's *The Fall of Berlin* (USSR, 1949), arguably the most fantastic icon in the entire cult of Stalin. Not only does Stalin appear in this film to have won the war almost singlehandedly, but he is portrayed as the liberator of the German people from the shackles of Nazism. Given that by this time Soviet film production was almost nil, this piece attracted starved moviegoers to the theaters despite itself.

After Stalin's death in 1953, something unexpected began to happen in the cinematic arena. As a result of Khrushchev's encouragement to artists to begin exploring some of the shortcomings of Soviet society, signified by the publication of Ilia Erenburg's novel *The Thaw,* some prominent Soviet filmmakers began to tinker with the formulas of the World War II film. They stubbornly refused to use war material in the old, obvious way. Rather than making stylized epics in socialist realist fashion, a daring few fomented a quiet rebellion that would eventually have ramifications that they may not have imagined at the time. By reconfiguring the war film as a kind of camera drama and jettisoning the traditions of the socialist realist epic, these filmmakers did much more than revolutionize a genre. They redefined "war" for the Soviet public and produced the most honest histories of World War II available to the population.

The epic was one of the most unshakeable of all Soviet cinematic traditions. It was a staple of Soviet cinema from its earliest years to its very end, dominating screens for the last two decades of Stalinism, but continuing to be significant through the Brezhnev era. The epic came in many styles. It could be stylized, like Sergei Eisenstein's *October* (USSR, 1928) and *Aleksandr Nevskii* (USSR, 1938), or bombastically laudatory, like Vladimir Petrov's *Peter the First* (USSR, 1937, 1939), a two-part saga. "Early Brezhnev" brought Sergei Bondarchuk's overblown screen adaptation of a great Russian classic, Tolstoi's *War and Peace* (USSR, 1966); "late Brezhnev," Andrei Konchalovskii's equally overblown twentieth-century family saga *Siberiade* (USSR, 1979). Given this longstanding tradition and the inherent affinity of the subject of war to epic form, we would logically expect those films made after World War II to mirror star-studded Anglo-American epics like *The Longest Day* (U.S., 1962) (so very like a socialist realist movie). Instead, we see Soviet directors breaking with epic pseudo-realism. Soviet World War II films tended to be markedly antiutopian, never varying significantly from the pattern established during the period of cultural reawakening (known as the Thaw, after Erenburg's novel) that was part of Khrushchev's de-Stalinization campaign.

After Khrushchev's "Secret Speech" of 1956, the floodgates opened. At that time, Soviet filmmakers traded public issues for personal themes and made a series of "quiet" war films. These works—the most famous of which are Mikhail Kalatozov's *The Cranes Are Flying* (USSR, 1957); Grigorii Chukhrai's *The Ballad of a Soldier* (USSR, 1959); and the last of the first generation, Tarkovskii's *Ivan's Childhood*[4]—stress the psychological impact of the war on individuals, whose behavior deviates from that of the sturdy heroines and heroes of war-era and postwar propaganda.

Often far from heroic, these people are nonetheless sympathetic characters and achingly human, like the heroine in *The Cranes Are Flying,* who marries another while her soldier lover is at the front, or the protagonist of *The Ballad of a Soldier*, who spends his brief leave ineffectually trying to help his mother. *Ivan's Childhood* focuses on the lost childhood of an orphan boy. Emerging from the cultural void of thirty years of Stalinism, *The Cranes Are Flying, The Ballad of a Soldier*, and *Ivan's Childhood* created a sensation with the public and, surprisingly enough, have endured as minor masterpieces (*Cranes* and *Soldier* find special favor with student audiences even today). It is important to remember, however, that although their antiwar themes made them seem to some Western critics as yet more Soviet propaganda, peace activism was considered dissident behavior in the Soviet Union.[5] These movies cannot, therefore, be read as reflections of the dominant ideology, and all encountered varying degrees of censorship, even in that time of comparative cultural relaxation.

Unfortunately for Soviet artists, the Thaw was short-lived, over even before Khrushchev's ouster in 1964, and during the eighteen years of the Brezhnevian "stagnation," Soviet filmmakers frequently found their creative license curtailed.[6] Yet they continued to test the limits of socialist realism, now through experimentation with—rather than denial of—established forms. For example, the historical epic could be subverted to countercultural political ends, as Tarkovskii's *Andrei Rublev* (USSR, 1966) compellingly demonstrates.[7] Likewise, the social-problem film could be transformed into an exploration of personal concerns, as in Georgian director Lana Gogoberidze's *Several Interviews on Personal Questions* (USSR, 1978).

Directors continued to alter the style and content of the war film in order to offer subtle and sometimes not-so-subtle critiques of the official history of the war. In examples from the mid-1960s to the mid-1970s, like their predecessors of the Thaw, the atypical became typical. Common themes included collaboration, desperation, suicide—not determined heroism and saintly sacrifice.

At one time or another, all the important directors of the 1960s and 1970s tackled the subject, sometimes more than once, even though the institutional impediments (particularly censorship) were great. Larissa Shepitko and Aleksei German deserve special notice. Early in her brief but brilliant career, Shepitko turned to the war. *Wings*, her 1966 picture, features a finely crafted psychological portrait of a celebrated woman aviator who apparently commits suicide by the film's end, since the drabness of her postwar life cannot match the exhilaration of her war experiences. A decade later, in *The Ascent,* Shepitko's 1977 masterpiece, we see an uncompromising indictment of wartime collaboration—the most taboo of all subjects in official histories of the war. Shepitko shows Soviet citizens actively and passively collaborating with the Nazis to commit atrocities in Belorussia, executing pitiful refugees who, as "partisan terrorists," happen to be in the wrong place at the wrong time. *The Ascent* was shown abroad, but its distribution in the Soviet Union was extremely limited.

German, best known in the West for *My Friend Ivan Lapshin* (USSR, 1983), also treated the forbidden theme of the collaborator in *Trial on the Road* (USSR, 1971); even though German's protagonist returns to the partisans and dies an improbable hero, the film, shelved by the censors, was not released until 1986. Undeterred by this experience, German returned to the war genre in *Twenty Days Without War* (USSR, 1976), which records the journey of a reporter behind the front lines; here German, ever subversive, appears more interested in the civilian casualties than in soldiers or partisans.

Shepitko and German were the most celebrated artists who made war films in the 1970s, but a few directors who became politically important in the Gorbachev era also distinguished themselves in this genre. For example, the subject of Nikolai Gubenko's *War Orphans* (USSR, 1977) is the war's dislocations and the inability of the state to deal, physically or psychologically, with the multitude of lost and orphaned children left behind.[8] In the 1980s, Klimov's *Come and See* was the best of a series of feature films released in 1985 to commemorate the fortieth anniversary of Germany's surrender.[9] *Come and See* is unusual in combining the epic scope of the socialist realist film with the personal sensibilities that characterize most other works of the genre.

This brief survey requires a cautionary note. The number of works should not be exaggerated, nor should their impact. It is certainly not representative of what Soviet audiences were seeing—else the system would have failed sooner that it did! Few directors dared to take such chances and faced grave difficulties even if the films made it through production. And yet, this body of work is remarkable in terms of quality and thematic consistency, and it serves as testimony to the continuing engagement of filmmakers with the unanswered questions of the war.

Of all these films, I have chosen two for closer examination, one from each of the two post-Stalin generations of war films. Tarkovskii's *Ivan's*

Childhood and Klimov's *Come and See* are on the surface quite different, the latter as "large" and overwrought as the former is "small" and understated. Their juxtaposition is a most unexpected one, and their contrasts illuminate changes in Soviet culture and society over the two decades that separate them. Yet they do share a number of important attributes. They are both significant works by major directors; they were widely seen and talked about in the Soviet Union and, to a lesser extent, abroad; and they illustrate the remarkable thematic and formal continuities in the war genre over nearly a quarter-century, a period during which, as we now know, the Soviet Union was slowly expiring. Finally, taken together, they represent the beginning and end of the genre.[10]

Ivan's Childhood, Tarkovskii's first feature, is a brilliant representative of the war films of the Thaw period. In many ways, it is the definitive Soviet World War II film, since, as was so often the case, the viewer never sees any real battles. There is no narrative in the classical sense. The viewer first sees Ivan, a twelve-year-old orphan, returning from a reconnaissance mission. Ivan eventually finds his company after initial mishaps. The officers discuss his future amid scenes of the destruction. They set off with Ivan for a new combat zone, and Ivan fails to return from his mission.

Conflict in the post-Stalinist World War II film is not viewed as glorious. It destroys not only life, but promise, especially the unfulfilled promises of childhood and youth. Tarkovskii's war orphan is a preternaturally mature and determined young boy who engages in reconnaissance missions for the Soviet army. More adult than many in the army unit that befriends him, Ivan remains eerily intense and single-minded in his goal of fighting the Germans (though his dreams of childhood remind us of his youth). His soldier guardians, however, squabble over petty matters, vie for the affections of the lone woman on duty (a nurse), mourn their losses, worry about their young charge, and yet continue coldly to exploit Ivan's devotion to them and their mutual cause.

Ivan's severe demeanor and strict adherence to military codes of behavior and ethics conform to conventions established in films made during the war itself concerning children. The year 1944 saw the release of Lev Arnshtam's *Zoia,* the "true story" of an eighteen-year-old partisan girl who is executed by the Germans; Viktor Eisimont's *Once There Was a Girl,* (which has the same refrain); and Mikhail Romm's grueling *Girl No. 217,* concerning a Russian girl enslaved by a German family.[11] Yet as Tarkovskii constantly reminds us, through dreams and flashbacks, Ivan is still a child.[12] The beautiful opening sequence is in fact a dream (memory?): Ivan and his mother are out in the forest, where Ivan is thrilled to hear the sound of a cuckoo. When his mother is killed by a shot near their well, Ivan bolts awake, crying despairingly, "Mama!" At the moment, he is hiding out in a windmill in the war zone; the shot he heard was real. Similar dreamlike episodes are inserted several times, most notably at the end, where we see Ivan, who has been hanged by the Nazis. He is playing on a golden beach, happy for eternity. (The last time we see him alive "for real," he is struggling in the dark through a swamp, on a mission.)

The military is always secondary to the individual in the genre. Actual battles are never shown in *Ivan's Childhood;* Ivan's "family" is part of the regular army rather than the more idiosyncratic partisan forces, yet they do not fit our stereotypes. Not only are they not especially regimented, but they act autonomously throughout. Indeed, they have actually disobeyed direct orders in Ivan's final mission by taking the child with them once again. Although the work is unusually concise for a Soviet film, in eighty-seven minutes Tarkovskii succeeds in humanizing each of the soldiers, thereby giving war a human, rather than a heroic, face. No one talks about Communism.

Ivan's Childhood revealed a new Soviet style that attracted international attention (and an award at the 1963 Venice Film Festival) for its innovative camera work. Its intimacy is conveyed not only by plot and characterization, but also by its camera techniques, which lead the spectator right into the action. There are many close-up and low-angle shots; the camera tracks and tilts obtrusively; the editing is far from seamless. Lighting is dim, yet the images are gritty and often all too clear.

Tarkovskii's treatment of nature became a staple of the genre. The special Russian relationship to nature has been memorialized in countless works of literature in the nineteenth and twentieth centuries. Tarkovskii shows that the war destroyed this, too. Prewar Russia is soft, light, open; Russia at war is dark, dank, closed in. Meadows are transformed to fields of death; horizons are low and bleak. Russia is a wasteland, a nightmare.

Ivan's Childhood is more than a film about one boy's childhood; it is a film about the fate of all children during World War II. (Tarkovskii's use of the generic Russian name Ivan, the name given protagonists in most folktales, is one important clue.) But its universality at the end of the picture is evident, too, through Tarkovskii's use of newsreel footage of the Nazis and documentary records of their crimes. The company's young lieutenant inadvertently confirms Ivan's fate by finding his photograph among Nazi rubble at the end of the war. Ivan's face, defiant and childlike, stares out at us. Newsreel footage rolls. Since the text of the film has had no specific historical referrents to this juncture, the point is made all the clearer that Tarkovskii intends Ivan as a symbol of the war dead and Nazi war guilt. (Such overt symbolism, which seems heavy-handed to some Western critics, is actually gentle and poetic in the Soviet context.)

More than twenty years after his startling cinematic debut, Tarkovskii was dying of cancer in exile in France; his public legacy in the Soviet Union was mixed—too elusive, too "Western," too elitist. His legendary status within the Soviet film world was, however, unrivaled, and no director with artistic pretensions could make a war film without at least thinking about *Ivan's Childhood.* In the mid-1980s, two rebel filmmakers who would be in the vanguard of the Gorbachev revolution, Elem Klimov and Ales Adamovich, made *Come and See,* a film memorializing the dead from the 628 Belorussian villages destroyed in the war.[13]

On the surface, *Come and See* seems to be a rather conventional Soviet film: too long, too clichéd, too bombastic, too melodramatic, too *epic.* Over the course of 142 unrelentingly grim minutes, Florian (nicknamed Flor), a youth in his mid-teens, is made to join the partisans; abandoned, he finds his way back to his village in the company of the partisan leader's discarded teenage mistress. The villagers have been massacred, and Flor's mother and sisters are among the dead. He staggers off with a few survivors, who are carrying an effigy they have made of Hitler. The men are ambushed on a field as they milk a cow they have commandeered, and only Flor survives. An elderly peasant tries to lead him to safety as the Germans move in and massacre the inhabitants of *this* village, too. The partisans arrive (but *after* the debacle) and capture and execute some of the Germans responsible. Flor, one of a handful of survivors, rejoins the partisans.

In narrative terms, *Come and See* is shapeless, extremely predictable, and rather old-fashioned, especially in its ghoulish caricatures of German soldiers, but it is "conventional" in *our* terms (like a bad television miniseries about the Nazis). This brand of grandiosity is not in fact a convention of the post-Stalin war film and harkens back to the movies of the war itself. Looking below the surface, we see strong thematic and stylistic continuities with Tarkovskii's *Ivan.* Klimov's picture can, therefore, be considered the last Soviet World War II movie in more ways than one, reprising all the devices of the genre.

Unlike the purposeful, totally committed Ivan, Flor is an accidental participant in the war, a naive draftee. His mother, left alone with two small children, is unwilling to see her "man" go with the partisans, who at first glance seem more than a little sinister. (They are definitely portrayed as jaded and amoral.) Like any adolescent, though, Flor is thrilled by the prospect of using his gun, which he has dug up on the beach, and is disappointed when the partisans decide to leave him behind at camp. He is humbled by the savoir-faire of the commander's teenage lover, though they soon become equals when the fighting starts. The terrified children struggle to find some haven, but after the discovery of the massacre of his fellow villagers and especially after the death of the cow, Flor becomes progressively unhinged. By the end of the movie, his face has become a mask of terror, infinitely childlike and infinitely old at once—like Ivan when he went into his dream-trances. The overly long and exceptionally busy climactic scene showing Nazi preparations for the destruction of the second village becomes artistically excessive only if the viewer does not recognize that we are watching this *through* Flor's eyes. Cowering forgotten in the dust, the traumatized child becomes sole witness to a tragedy.

Klimov's partisans are certainly less than heroic, like the soldiers in *Ivan's Childhood,* but they are also much less sympathetic. Everyone in *Come and See* seems to have lost the sense of right and wrong in the chaos of war—markedly different from *Ivan's Childhood* and reflecting, arguably, the hopelessness of the early 1980s in the Soviet Union. The Belorussian peasants are preyed on by all sides. Flor and his new pals steal the cow for their own purposes, not for the war, as they claim self-servingly. Nowhere, however, is this amorality clearer than at the end, when the partisans are trying to decide what to do with the captured Germans. Several men want to torture them; one douses them with gasoline and prepares to set them on fire. Suddenly the commander, remembering that he is a representative of the Red Army (which does not, of course, countenance terror and torture), orders them shot. Disappointed, the lynch mob dissipates, and the partisans head into the forest once again.

Stylistically, there are clear differences between the two motion pictures. For example, the scale of Klimov's film is much bigger than that of Tarkovskii's; wide-screen CinemaScope suits its breadth and length. And yet there are strong similarities as well. *Come and See* is surprisingly intimate, due to close-ups, low-angle shots, and the constantly moving but slightly (and deliberately) amateurish camerawork. *Come and See* also features a ruined and ominous landscape, filmed in muddy color on grainy film stock. Although titles proclaim that this picture is based on the true story of the sack and massacre of the Belorussian village of Khatyn (and, indeed, Adamovich's screenplay was based on his interviews with survivors), nothing really distinguishes the location from that of any Soviet village.

The use of actual footage at the end, which mimics the ending of *Ivan's Childhood,* is noteworthy. After the execution of the captured Germans, Flor becomes transfixed by a portrait of Hitler floating in a pool of water. He begins shooting at it. As he shoots (far too many rounds for his gun without reloading), we see Hitler's life unfolding in reverse, until we get to the final picture, a still portrait of Hitler as a baby in his mother's arms. Flor hesitates, puts his gun down, and runs to join the partisans.

Flor lives, Ivan dies, yet *Come and See* is undeniably a more despairing and negative film than *Ivan's Childhood*—and not because it is more graphic about the terror and atrocities of the war. Anna Lawton has dubbed *Come and See* an "apocalyptic" movie;[14] indeed, its pervasive pessimism certainly may be seen as a cinematic reflection of the Soviet public's morale near the end of the regime. No one believes in the cause in *Come and See;* no one seems to understand it. All humanity has degenerated, although the Germans are undeniably much worse than others. The end is the ultimate enigma—and therefore the ultimate challenge to a state that could not tolerate uncertainty and ambiguity. Was Flor right not to kill the baby Hitler? *Could* he have? Would anything have changed had he done so?

Perhaps nobody dares answer that question. Without closer examination of the style and content of all the post-Stalin World War II films, it would be premature to conclude too much from a brief and selective analysis of the genre. But one can point out a few issues that the "radical fringe" of this genre, as embodied in these two films, denotes in the complicated history of Soviet cultural politics.

Stalin admired and feared art for the same reason: he recognized its power to mobilize public opinion and to subvert state policies. He knew how to manipulate art as have few others. He was a master at mythmaking, and he lay the foundations for the myth of the Great Fatherland War while the war itself was in progress and before he knew that its outcome would match up to the advance billing. Movies were central to his vision of justifying the terrible losses of the war as a tribute to Soviet courage and patriotism, rather than as a reflection of his own monumental errors.

The best Soviet directors were cultural rebels. In the 1920s, they were loud; in the 1960s and after, quiet. Given the pervasiveness of the World War II myth, with its monuments and graveyards and medals and parades; given its political necessity as a stabilizing force after Stalin's death—puncturing its hollow heart (as did Tarkovskii and Klimov) was a profoundly subversive act. Not only was war not heroic, but the Great Fatherland War, *as constructed by the regime,* mocked the nation's true sacrifices and nobility. The Soviet war film became, in effect, a counter-analysis of official history.

In a very real way, then, Soviet directors were the historians of their generation, the chroniclers of the last thirty years of Soviet power. Moreover, through these movies it is evident that autonomous action *was* possible in late Soviet society, even from those working within the system. We can also see the role that film directors played in eroding—slowly but persistently—the foundations of the state. Finally, as profoundly as these films subverted the myth of a glorious, heroic war, they stand as warnings against the dangers of forgetting. Why else would Klimov and Adamovich have exhorted us to "come and see"?

NOTES

The author wishes to thank Frank Manchel for his astute critique of an earlier draft of this chapter.

1. The cultural and social ramifications of the war have been virtually unexplored. Instead, the overwhelming majority of the hundreds of books on the subject have been military or diplomatic histories. For contemporary exceptions, see John Garrard and Carol Garrard, eds., *World War II and the Soviet People* (New York: St. Martin's Press, 1992); and John Barber and Mark Harrison, *The Soviet Home Front: A Social and Economic History of the USSR in World War II* (London: Longman, 1992). The works most closely related to the subject of this chapter, however, are Nina Tumarkin's idiosyncratic but interesting examination of the war cult, *The Living and the Dead: The Rise and Fall of the Cult of World War II in Russia* (New York: Basic Books, 1994); and Richard Stites, ed., *Culture and Entertainment in Wartime Russia* (Bloomington: Indiana University Press, 1995).

2. For the only scholarly surveys in English on this subject, see Peter Kenez, *Cinema and Soviet Society, 1917–1953* (New York: Cambridge University Press, 1992), chap. 9; and Richard Stites, *Russian Popular Culture: Entertainment and Society Since*

1900 (Cambridge: Cambridge University Press, 1992), chap. 4. Tumarkin, in *Living and the Dead,* covers literature extensively, but pays scant attention to film.

3. *She Defends Her Motherland* was released in the United States as *No Greater Love,* a typical example of American retitling to emphasize the personal over the political. This film and other heroine films are discussed in Francoise Navailh, "The Emancipated Woman: Stalinist Propaganda in Soviet Feature Film, 1930–1950," *Historical Journal of Film, Radio and Television* 12, no. 3 (1992): 208–10.

4. *Ivan's Childhood* became *My Name Is Ivan* in its U.S. release, an especially senseless example of retitling.

5. For a contemporary example of "old-style" Soviet criticism that makes these movies sound like what they are not—that is, glorification of war—see Rostislav Iurenev, *Kratkaia istoriia sovetskogo kino* (Moscow: Biuro propagandy sovetskogo kinoiskusstvo, 1979), pp. 195–97 (in English, the section is entitled "Heroes of the Great War"). For a more "enlightened" discussion of the Thaw, also by a Soviet film historian (but written for the Western audience at the end of the *glasnost* era), see Neya Zorkaya, *The Illustrated History of Soviet Cinema* (New York: Hippocrene Books, 1989), chap. 5.

6. For a discussion of the cinema of the Brezhnev era, see Anna Lawton, *Kinoglasnost: Soviet Cinema in Our Time* (Cambridge: Cambridge University Press, 1992).

7. Denise J. Youngblood, "Post-Utopian History as Art and Politics: Andrei Tarkovskii's *Andrei Rublev,*" in *The Persistence of History: Cinema, Television, and the Modern Event,* ed. Vivian Sobchack (New York: Routledge, 1995).

8. It is worth noting that Nikolai Gubenko, a gifted actor and theater director, became Gorbachev's last minister of culture, yet another indication of the influence later enjoyed by makers of such films.

9. Elem Klimov is the widower of Larissa Shepitko, who died in an automobile accident in 1979.

10. There is a brief discussion of *Come and See* in Lawton, *Kinoglasnost,* pp. 225–26. For *Ivan's Childhood,* see Zorkaya, *Illustrated History of Soviet Cinema,* pp. 232–33; and Vida T. Johnson and Graham Petrie, *The Films of Andrei Tarkovsky: A Visual Fugue* (Bloomington: Indiana University Press, 1994), pp. 62–78.

11. See the ever-reliable Jay Leyda, *Kino: A History of the Russian and Soviet Film* (London: George Allen and Unwin, 1960), chap. 17.

12. Johnson and Petrie, *Films of Andrei Tarkovsky,* focus on the dream sequences in their analysis of the film.

13. Klimov and the late Ales Adamovich became important political figures in the Gorbachev era, contributing in significant ways to *perestroika* in the film industry. Adamovich, who died of a heart attack on January 26, 1994, was a well-known and outspoken supporter of radical democratic reform.

14. Lawton, *Kinoglasnost,* p. 225.

6

The Longest Day (U.S., 1962): "Blockbuster" History

STEPHEN E. AMBROSE

The Longest Day (U.S., 1962) is one of my favorite historical films. I can still recall the sense of pride when I walked out of the theater in the fall of 1962 after seeing it for the first time. *The Longest Day* helps us visualize the scale and drama of the Allied invasion of Normandy on June 6, 1944, an invasion that marked the beginning of the end of Nazi control in Western Europe. This enormous three-hour film is one of the great epics about World War II. A true "blockbuster," it powerfully re-created on a grand scale the largest amphibious invasion in history. The deployment of thousands of troops, a vast quantity of battle equipment, and the wizardry of exploding shells resulted in Academy Awards for cinematography and special effects.

This film was based on Cornelius Ryan's enormously successful book of the same title (800,000 copies sold in the first year). Ryan had covered the Normandy invasion in 1944 for the London *Daily Telegraph*. Later, over the course of a decade, he interviewed nearly 1,000 survivors for the book in which he ingeniously combined personal reminiscences with a compelling account of the invasion.[1] How to use those numerous individual stories within a coherent and integrated story line was one of the major challenges faced by the filmmakers. It was a challenge they never quite met. The other major challenge, of course, was re-creating the spectacle of the largest amphibious invasion force in history. In this, the filmmakers were tremendously successful. As an epic spectacle of the turning point in the war in the West, *The Longest Day* remains one of Hollywood's most remarkable logistical achievements.

On D-Day, June 6, 1944, an invasion force composed primarily of American, British, and Canadian troops numbered nearly 175,000 men, more than 3,000 ships and landing craft, and thousands of aircraft that flew some 14,000 sorties.[2] After the initial beachhead was secured on the first day and the Allies had gotten past the Germans' primary line of defense, the fortifications of the so-called Atlantic Wall, more than 1 million Allied troops surged into France within a month.

Dubbed "The Longest Film" by some critics, the 180–minute epic was the largest and most expensive war film made up to that time. It had cost nearly $10 million by the time it premiered on October 1, 1962. It was also the most expensive black-and-white motion picture. The driving force was Darryl F. Zanuck, one of Hollywood's toughest moguls and longtime executive at twentieth Century–Fox. He had previously been responsible for such war films as *Drums Along the Mohawk* (U.S., 1939) from the American Indian wars and *Twelve O'Clock High* (U.S., 1951), concerning the Allied bombing campaign against Germany. Zanuck hired three directors, Ken Annakin, Andrew Marton, and Bernhard Wicki, and directed several major scenes himself. Elmo Williams coordinated the battle scenes.

The Longest Day is the bane of American historians of D-Day because, ever since, to the average audience, you must identify the men you are talking about not by their names but by the actors who played them. People look puzzled when I mention General Cota, but when I say, "You know, Robert Mitchum," they nod knowingly; no one recognizes Lieutenant Colonel Vandervoort's name, but when I say, "You know, John Wayne," everyone knows.

Zanuck's decision to cast famous stars as not only the principal historical figures of the invasion but even in cameo appearances as average soldiers had great audience appeal. The countless stars, the major spectacle of so many people and so much equipment, dynamic special effects, and faithful reproduction in moving images of many of the still photographs of the actual invasion helped make *The Longest Day* a major success at the box office. It grossed $17.5 million, nearly double the original cost.

This film reinforces one patriotic theme: the triumph of democracy over dictatorship. The American, British, and Canadian soldiers are bold, eager to take the initiative, and confident in their leaders and in their cause, while the German soldiers are confused, fearful of seizing opportunities, and deeply suspicious of the cause they serve. The theme is underscored visually by the scenes of the immense fleets behind the invading soldiers—a miracle of industrial production that expressed perfectly General Dwight Eisenhower's 1942 warning: "Beware the fury of an aroused democracy."

Viewers know that most of what they see really happened. In the credits, the movie hammers the point home, with a long list of military consultants, including some of D-Day's most famous men.

The film was intended to commemorate the approaching twentieth anniversary of the invasion. But the real explanation for Zanuck's interest is evident from a glimpse of twentieth Century–Fox's financial difficulties, particularly the colossal losses associated with *Cleopatra* (U.S., 1960). For Zanuck, sixty years old in 1962, it was up or out. He paid $175,000 for the screen rights to Ryan's book. Before he was done, he had five scriptwriters, including Ryan, Romain Gary, and James Jones; a battle-scenes coordinator; thirty-seven military advisers; and forty-two stars for speaking parts. Audiences were overwhelmed by the number of genuine stars assembled for one film, including John Wayne, Robert Mitchum, Henry Fonda, Robert Ryan, Rod Steiger, Robert Wagner, Mel Ferrer, Jeffrey Hunter, Paul Anka, Sal Mineo, Roddy McDowall, Eddie Albert, Edmund O'Brien, Fabian, Red Buttons, Richard Burton, Kenneth More, Peter Lawford, Richard Todd, Leo Genn, Sean Connery, and Curt Jurgens.

Zanuck justified his use of so many stars in terms of showmanship: "I wanted the audience to have a kick. Every time a door opened, in would come a famous star."[3] But another explanation turns as well on a story with so many characters. There would be action by dozens of men and units. How could an audience keep everything straight or remember what they had seen? The solution was simple: Lieutenant Colonel Vandervoort was played by John Wayne. In a particularly nice casting touch, Richard Todd played Major John Howard, whose glider-borne company had began the battle. In 1944, Todd was a paratrooper on D-Day who ended up fighting in Howard's company. Because *The Longest Day* covered only twenty-four hours on a limited front of some sixty miles, it lent itself to the blurring between fiction and actuality. If Wayne equaled Vandervoort in viewer's minds, it did not mean viewers thought Wayne actually helped lead the D-Day invasion.

Accuracy of detail is explained by Zanuck's willingness to take the advice of so many military advisers. They made an impressive roster: General James Gavin, Lord Lovat, Major John Howard, Commander H. J. Kieffer of the French commandos, General Pierre Koenig of the Free

French forces, Admiral Friedrich Ruge of the German navy, Lucie Rommel (wife of the "Desert Fox"), and others.

Two decisions by Zanuck particularly affected the final outcome. One was to shoot in black-and-white. (As one of my students told me, "World War II? Isn't that the one they fought in black-and-white?") The second was to have the characters speak in their own languages (English, French, or German), with the use of subtitles.

The decision to shoot in black-and-white saved a good deal of money. Zanuck also saved money when it came to military advisers. He did not pay them. He did, however, throw wonderful parties, including dinner parties. Howard recalls being treated like royalty while he was in France (with his wife), serving as technical adviser for the opening combat scene at Pegasus Bridge. Zanuck put the advisers in the best hotels. The old veterans mingling together was a symbol of the reconciliation between Germany and the Allies, as was the movie itself.

Howard told me, however, that the military advisers were not always listened to. On D-Day night, Howard's first task had been to seize the bridge before it could be blown—it was known to be prepared for demolition in the event of a raid by the French Resistance. Once the bridge was secure, his immediate task was to search for and remove the explosives thought to be in place under the girders. Howard accomplished his objectives, but his engineers found no explosives under the bridge. They were in a nearby shed, not in place but ready to be moved.

The engineers reported to Howard that there were no charges under the bridge. Welcome news to Howard in 1944. But not to Zanuck in 1962. The producer insisted that there *had* to be explosives in place so his engineer stuntmen could do their hand-over-hand movement from the bank of the canal to the girders, remove the charges, and throw them into the water. The scene was shot as Zanuck wanted it, with Howard looking on in disbelief.

The worst distortion took place on Omaha Beach. The generals' original invasion plan in 1944 had been for bulldozers to open the "exits" from the beaches, so that tanks could drive up the draw and get to the top of the bluff. The infantry would follow. That plan was a bust within minutes. For the tanks did not make it ashore, nor did the bulldozers, and the "exits" were heavily fortified, to the point of being impregnable to attack from the front or sides. They were vulnerable from the rear, however. That meant the infantrymen had to work their way up the bluff, and then come down on the fortifications from behind. And that is what happened.

Junior officers or non-commissioned officers took charge and led their infantrymen up and around and down behind the German fortifications. It was individual initiative and democracy at its best. But it was not the dramatic episode Zanuck wanted.

Perhaps Zanuck had too many generals among his advisers, and too few enlisted men. More likely, Zanuck decided that the image of a few groups of men going up a bluff and crawling down behind the enemy line just did not provide a powerful visual impact. He wanted a final big bang. Whatever the reason, the climax to the movie comes when the cement barrier is blown up, the rubble cleared, and the men of the First and Twenty-ninth Divisions come rushing from behind the sea wall and, in a grand climatic charge, dash through the hole and up the bluff. It makes a great scene. It is what movie viewers presumably expect. Unfortunately, nothing remotely like it ever happened on D-Day. Such artistic license did not bother Zanuck in the least. His reply to such criticism was: "Anything changed was an asset to the film. There is nothing duller on the screen than being accurate but not dramatic."[4]

Surprisingly, in one instance Zanuck downplayed a scene. It is one of the most memorable in the movie. Shortly after midnight, Private John Steele (Red Buttons) hangs helplessly in his parachute, which is caught on the steeple of the church in Sainte-Mere-Eglise. He watches, horrified, as a firefight with Germans in the village square wipes out his buddies.

That was the scene in the film, but there was more to it than that, though Zanuck did not know it. In 1944, there was a second paratrooper caught on that church, hanging helplessly. His name was Ken Russell, and he told his story in a 1988 interview. Russell saw his buddies being sucked into the fire in the barn near the square. He jerked on his parachute risers to avoid it and came down on the slate roof of the church: "I hit and a couple of my suspension lines went around the church steeple and I slid off the roof. I was hanging off the edge. And Steele, he came down and his chute covered the steeple."

Sergeant John Ray landed in the church square, just past Russell and Steele. A German soldier came around the corner. "I'll never forget him," Russell related. "He was red-haired, and as he came around he shot Sergeant Ray in the stomach. Then he turned toward me and Steele and brought his machine pistol up to shoot us. And Sergeant Ray, while he was dying in agony, he got his .45 out and he shot the German soldier in the back of the head and killed him."

If Zanuck failed to include the drama of Sainte-Mere-Eglise, he made up for it with other out-and-out inventions. The one that most distresses veterans who were in the invasion involves men coming off the Higgins boats—the smallest landing craft—each carrying thirty-two men. In the movie, they leap into the water, rush through the waves, dash across the beach, throw themselves behind the sea wall, and start firing at the enemy. In reality, they plunged in over their heads, inflated their life jackets, struggled to shore, hid behind beach obstacles, crawled forward to the sea wall, and threw themselves down, exhausted.

Another deception involves the depiction of death. Lots of men are killed in the movie, but always in a clean shot that brings instant death. There are no wounds to speak of, no blood, no scenes depicting the true price of war, the damage that bullets and high explosives can do to the human body. In this sense, the movie is so far remote from reality that it seems little more than Hollywood fantasy.

By contrast, Madame Gondree helped Zanuck stick a bit closer to reality. She and her husband ran the Gondree Café at the Pegasus Bridge. It was the first building liberated in France. The Gondrees, who were in the French Resistance, helped the British paratroopers through D-Day. The couple had small children. An irresistible subject, made even more so by the on-site filming opportunity: the café was charmingly French, and unchanged since 1944 (and still unchanged in 1994).

These facts, and her own personality, made it possible for Madame Gondree to stand up to Zanuck. During the occupation, the Gondrees had served members of the local German garrison in their café (they passed on to England information they gained by eavesdropping on the conversation, since Madame Gondree understood German, unbeknownst to the Germans). The Gondrees had kept German soldiers from being billeted in their home by giving each of their small daughters her own room, thus having none to spare.

The attack on the bridge and café is the opening action sequence in the movie. It was a memorable piece of high drama in 1944 and again in 1962 in *The Longest Day*. Zanuck wanted to improve on it. When the café came under fire, he wanted half-dressed German soldiers jumping out of the windows of the Gondree Café. But when Zanuck started to shoot the scene, Madame Gondree insisted that she had *never* had any Germans sleeping in her house. Zanuck, she insisted, had to take that scene out of the script. Zanuck had no choice but to surrender lest he lose the right to film in the café.

When it came to equipment, however, Zanuck insisted on complete authenticity. In 1962, there were no Horsa gliders, such as Howard and his men had used, so Zanuck got the blueprints and had one built in Britain. The Air Ministry claimed that the design was inherently bad, that the glider was not airworthy (something that the thousands of men who crossed the English Channel in hundreds of the craft would have been surprised to learn), and that therefore Zanuck could not have a permit to tow it by air across the Channel, as he had hoped to do. He dismantled the Horsa, brought it over by ship, and put it together again in France.

Generally, Zanuck tried to get his equipment and his troops for free, or as close to free as possible. Here he was able to capitalize on the pride in D-Day felt by the armed forces of the Allied nations. The U.S. Army in Germany and the U.S. Sixth Fleet let Zanuck hire several thousand soldiers and twenty-two ships for a pittance. The British provided 1,000 paratroopers almost without cost; the French donated 2,000 infantrymen, some of whom donned GI uniforms. The U.S. military supplied Zanuck with jeeps, tanks, and armored halftracks, plus hundreds of assorted landing craft.

Mitchum (playing General Cota) got himself into some trouble when he told an interviewer that some of the American GIs from the U.S. Army in Germany had been afraid to board a landing craft: "It was raining, the wind was blowing, the sea was rough, and these troops were afraid to board. I had to hop aboard first myself with some other actors and stuntmen before they gave in."

In 1962, Zanuck offered a vivid description of the logistics involved in shooting such an enormous spectacle:

> From the beginning I had 2 units shooting film simultaneously, and at times there were 4. It made it very difficult for me, but everything had been worked out in advance, in great detail, and I used a helicopter to drop in on my directors and supervise the work being done.
>
> Only about one-third of *The Longest Day* was shot in the studio. When we did move indoors, I took over the Studio Boulogne—France's largest—for 3 months. We built 47 separate sets there. Here, too, I had 2 units working simultaneously on different stages. At the studio we reproduced everything from the interior of a glider and of a landing craft at sea (the motions were simulated by having the craft built on a platform that sank and rose with hydraulic pressure) to the Normandy countryside and the interior of a German bunker under bombardment. One scene called for Irina Demich to fight a German soldier in the water. It was freezing out, so we couldn't shoot in the country. I had a stream built on the stage and the water was preheated to keep her and everyone else from catching pneumonia.[5]

Not everyone loved *The Longest Day*. Critic Basil Wright dismissed the "would-be super blockbuster" as "singularly unmemorable."[6] *Time* magazine was unhappy with the film—too many lines, too many actors, too little direction—and predicted that it would not make back the $10 million cost. D-Day "must some day find its Homer," the reviewer noted. "At the moment, it has Darryl Zanuck."[7]

However, critic Bosley Crowther of the *New York Times* could not restrain himself. Publicists at twentieth Century–Fox might have blushed to have written such a review themselves. Highly suspenseful, exciting, smashing, a perfect blend of history and drama, breathtaking were but a few of his words of praise. He concluded, "The total effect of the picture is that of a huge documentary report, adorned and colored by personal details that are thrilling, amusing, ironic, sad."[8]

Newsweek disagreed. It called the movie a "pseudodocumentary" and complained that "there are no heroes. This man is brave for ten seconds and that man lovable for five, but the individuals are only incidental. . . . D-Day, itself, is the only real subject." Zanuck could rightly have read that last comment as praise. He had put nearly four dozen genuine stars in the movie and gotten away with it—D-Day itself remained his subject. "The film is dazzled by its own size," the *Newsweek* reviewer concluded, "and finally seems convinced that size alone is enough. D-Day was, admittedly, quite large. It was also a terrible day, and a terribly necessary day. The picture should have confronted those truths, too, for without them, it is all a swarm of human lemmings going the wrong way."[9]

The *Saturday Review* writer complained about "preposterous dialogue."[10] This is a major problem in war movies: How do you explain to the audience what is going on without maps and a voiceover? Zanuck's script made the actors carry the story line. For example, before boarding for the flight across, Robert Ryan as General James Gavin and John Wayne as Lieutenant Colonel Vandervoort have a conversation that amounts to a basic orientation course on the airborne landings in Normandy. No military historian believes they ever had such a simplistic conversation. Such touches, necessary to comprehend what is going on, inevitably weaken the presumptive accuracy of the film. The *New Yorker* magazine was highly critical. "It struck me as I watched the Zanuck juggernaut," its reviewer noted, "that the fumbling of the German High Command upon discovering the Allied armada off the Norman beaches was being played, at least in part, for laughs."[11] Actually, Zanuck's portrayal of the indecisive German high command was one of the most accurate parts of his film. By way of contrast, there were inaccuracies in who did what. For example, Brigadier General Theodore Roosevelt, Jr., who had landed a mile south of his planned point of attack on Utah Beach, immediately jettisoned the plans: "We'll start the war from right here." Never mind that in reality Colonel James Van Fleet made the decision; the point was that the Allied commanders at various levels were not afraid to act on their own.

This film endorses not only the superiority of the Allied forces, but also the natural leadership and bearing of officers portrayed as distant leaders at command headquarters (such as Henry Fonda as Brigadier General Roosevelt), noble but lonely in their isolation from their troops, or battle leaders on the front lines with their troops (Wayne, Mitchum), courageous, patriotic, but also fatherly in their concern for their men.

The Longest Day, as Christine Diligenti-Gavriline notes in an illuminating essay, was made long enough after the end of World War II to allow Zanuck to depict the German soldiers with relative impartiality.[12] By 1962, the war had been over for nearly two decades; West Germany had been rearmed and brought into the NATO alliance to block a possible invasion by the Soviet Union. A larger purpose of the film, thus, was to show reconciliation among the Germans, British, French, and Americans, now acting together against a Communist threat from the east.

This purpose led to the sympathetic portrayal of a number of German soldiers, including General Erwin Rommel. Zanuck consulted with Rommel's widow less to ensure accuracy than to underscore how Rommel, connected to the July 20, 1944, plot to kill Hitler, became in death a martyr for the German resistance. The destruction of Nazism required that Germany be defeated; by making most of the enemy soldiers simply Germans rather than Nazis, *The Longest Day* offered a kind of exculpation in 1962 for a worthy, chastened, and now useful former foe. In the film, General Günther Blumentritt (played by Curt Jurgens) offers a justification of German failure: "We are disillusioned witnesses of a fact that will seem hard to believe to future historians, but it is still the truth: No one must wake up the Führer." Hitler's deficiencies, Jurgens implied, alone explain the failure of the Germans to repulse the D-Day landings.

One can note in passing that the refusal, in June 1994, to allow the Germans to participate in the fiftieth-anniversary celebrations of D-Day suggests that Zanuck felt a greater forgiveness in 1962 than what proved possible today, thirty years *after* the film was made. But such a comment can also be misleading. Darryl Zanuck was making a giant Hollywood extravaganza, not orchestrating public memory. Nor did Zanuck have to coordinate several governments over the final massive return of the remaining veterans who fought on D-Day.

NOTES

1. Cornelius Ryan, *The Longest Day* (New York: Simon and Schuster, 1959). Ryan prided himself on his factual accuracy, but did insist that a crucial skirmish took place at Ouistreham Casino, which in fact had been destroyed by an RAF bombing raid in 1942. See Lawrence H. Suid, *Guts & Glory: Great American War Movies* (Reading, Mass.: Addison-Wesley, 1978), p. 149.

2. Stephen E. Ambrose, *D-Day: The Climatic Battle of World War II* (New York: Simon and Schuster, 1994), pp. 239, 257, 576.

3. Leonard Mosley, *Zanuck: The Rise and Fall of Hollywood's Last Mogul* (Boston: Little, Brown, 1984), p. 346.

4. Darryl F. Zanuck, quoted in Suid, *Guts & Glory,* pp. 149–50.

5. Zanuck, interview in *Films & Filming,* November 1962, reprinted in Jay Leyda, *Voices of Film Experience, 1894 to the Present* (New York: Macmillan, 1977), p. 519.

6. Basil Wright, *The Long View* (London: Paladin, 1976), p. 628.

7. "Operation Overblown," *Time,* October 19, 1962, p. 91.

8. Bosley Crowther, "Screen: Premiere of 'The Longest Day,' " *New York Times,* October 5, 1962, p. A28.

9. "No Blood, No Cries," *Newsweek,* October 15, 1962, p. 105.

10. Hollis Alpert, "Size and Sweep," *Saturday Review,* October 20, 1962, p. 34.

11. "Under Fire" *New Yorker,* October 13, 1962, p. 188.

12. Christine Diligenti-Gavriline, "Reproachless Heroes of World War II: A Cinematic Approach Through Two American Movies," in "Guerra, cinema i societat" [special issue], ed. J. M. Caparros-Lera, Sergi Alegre, and Luis Anyo, *Film Historia* 3, nos. 1, 2 (1993): 55–64.

7

The Life and Times of Rosie the Riveter (U.S., 1980): The Experience and Legacy of Wartime Women Wage Earners

ALICE KESSLER-HARRIS

In 1946, the distinguished anthropologist Margaret Mead sought to evaluate the experiences of American women during World War II. Not much had happened, she concluded. Some women had moved in or stayed with parents; others had moved somewhat. Some who might not otherwise have done so had gone to work, and others, already working, had taken jobs that had been closed to them before the war. A few (perhaps 250,000) had entered the armed services. But all told, these changes did not add up to much. Women, Mead concluded, would now know a bit more about unions and be a little more empathetic to their husband's trials at work. "Most of all women have waited. . . . [T]hey have learned to live . . . on the memory of a few short days. . . . to value love and marriage . . . more."[1] In short, American women, having suffered no important and catastrophic hardships, were asked "to go on living pretty much as they did before."[2] The only catch was that their men had changed, and women might have a hard time figuring them out.

A year later, a well-known psychiatrist, Marynia F. Farnham, and her collaborator, Ferdinand Lundberg, sharply disagreed with Mead's assessment. In their view, the war had been a disaster for women. In *Modern Woman: The Lost Sex,* a book that rapidly became a best-seller, they diagnosed the condition of modern woman as deplorable. Industrial civilization, fueled by war and the wartime experience, had deprived women of their "sphere of creative nurture"—a sphere formerly satisfied by home and family. It was up to society, they argued, to attract women "into organizing their lives more closely around the home."[3] Their suggestions for implementing change were quite concrete. Among other things, they advocated removing spinsters from teaching jobs lest they offer "inadequate models of complete women," allowing married women to work only part time, and, depriving households of mechanical gadgets that invaded women's functions and deprived them of their meaning.[4] For the health of society and its children, American women, according to Farnham and Lundberg, should be restored to their proper work of nurturing.

The psychologists, anthropologists, and sociologists engaged in this postwar debate were concerned with far more than the fate of women. At stake were the broader values of American culture that rotated around the family and the home. Experts wondered whether women had left the home in such significant numbers and with sufficiently satisfying results to undermine forever their desire to return. Or had women left temporarily and reluctantly in response to national crisis, eager to resume their home lives when the war ended? Would the war, in short, encourage women to alter permanently their stance toward earning a living and thus inevitably change their relationship to husbands, family, and the meaning of the home?

The debate among social scientists in the 1940s has continued unabated, echoed by historians influenced by the emergence of the women's liberation movement of the late 1960s and the 1970s. Like the earlier debate, the substance of the current disagreement among historians is over whether the war encouraged women to alter permanently their stance toward the home.[5] But unlike the experts of the 1940s who tried to minimize the influence of the war and who held women responsible for its effects, later scholars have explored how the shape of World War II—its language, metaphors, demands, and restrictions—altered perceptions of gender roles in ways that encouraged women to contest traditional definitions of wage work and family life and to expand their meanings.[6]

In this debate, Connie Field's prize-winning film, *The Life and Times of Rosie the Riveter* (U.S., 1980),[7] figures prominently. Since its New York Film Festival debut in September 1980, it has become not just a documentary about the impact of the war on women, but a document whose visual and written texts shape perceptions of women's historical experience and reinforce current arguments in favor of gender equity. Field fully intended this result for her first feature film. She set out, she tells us, to make a film that would debunk what she calls the myth that middle-class women

Norman Rockwell's famous illustration of "Rosie the Riveter" for the cover of the *Saturday Evening Post,* May 29, 1943. (Printed by permission of the Norman Rockwell Family Trust. Copyright ©1943 the Norman Rockwell Family Trust)

entered the war plants for patriotic reasons. Instead, she sought out working-class women whose prewar work in unsatisfying and poorly paid jobs had led them to look on the war as a great opportunity. To find her protagonists, she interviewed some 700 women from San Francisco, Los Angeles, and Detroit. Field, who had completed a master's degree in women's history two years before she started the film, and who was active in the women's movement, viewed filmmaking "as part of a process of social communication and change."[8]

The Life and Times of Rosie the Riveter has certainly served that function. Within a year of its release, it had been seen by more than a million people,[9] including, according to the *New York Times,* scores of labor, community, church, school, and women's groups.[10] Dubbed into six languages, it won acclaim and prizes at film festivals all over Europe. Its influence has been felt in such commercial productions as *Swing Shift* (U.S., 1984), a Hollywood motion picture produced by and starring Goldie Hawn. Some commentators consider the five women around whose memories the film pivots as representative of the wartime experience of women wage earners.[11]

Field uses a simple technique to make a lasting point. She intercuts newsreel clips and excerpts from recruitment films of the 1940s with interviews with five women who had obtained good jobs during the war and lost them at its end. The clips present the official line about such issues as why women should join the workforce (to help win the war) and what to expect afterward (to go home to their families).

In contrast, the five on-camera "Rosies" speak about their hunger for economic opportunity and their eagerness to remain in the good jobs they felt they had earned. Each is superbly appropriate. Two of the five are white—both working class, one from an urban, and the other from a rural, setting. Lola Weixel, just married when the war began, had worked in a toy factory. Her Brooklyn family had participated in union organizing campaigns during the Depression, so she knew how to recognize unfair treatment in the workforce. Gladys Belcher grew up working on a farm, so she was totally comfortable around machinery when she responded to the call of the shipyards. The three African-American women had been domestic day workers—reflecting the discriminatory job market faced by women of color. Each had to solve a major child-care problem to enter war work. Wanita Allen, separated from her husband for many years, sent her teenage daughters off to boarding school. Margaret Wright moved from Detroit to California with her small child to get the industrial training she would need. Lynn Childs left her young daughter with her mother in Los Angeles when she found training and work in a Richmond, California, shipyard.

Memories of personal accomplishment mixed with bitter disappointment permeate the tales of all five women. Weixel, trained to weld bomb casings, thought she might use her skills by turning to making ornamental iron gates at war's end. Not so. Belcher could plow fields like a man before she became a welder, but she lost her new job when the war was over. Allen had left a restaurant kitchen to work in a Detroit foundry, but afterward found herself back in the kitchen. Wright moved from domestic service to munitions work and back to domestic service within the space of five years. Childs beat out all her white colleagues for a precious welding job as a ship's burner, which she held to the war's end. After 1945, all found themselves back in jobs traditionally reserved for women.

Drawing much of its power from the moving stories of these five heroines, the film offers a persuasive confrontation between memory (which is depicted as truth) and World War II–era film clips and other visual images (which appear to the contemporary viewer as irony). The irony is heightened by the realities of American society in 1980, when the film was released. Caught in an inflationary cycle that made it increasingly difficult for families to survive on a single income, prepared by high levels of education to enter the labor force, inspired toward economic independence by the rhetoric of a revivified women's movement, record numbers of women were earning wages. Many responded to the ideology of fairness and equity that justified their new roles—but many also suffered from widespread sexual and racial discrimination. Caught between a discourse of equality and the experience of discrimination, women responded to the film's re-creation of the long forgotten World War II experience as a reflection of their own current problems.

The battle on-screen between official memory and personal experience is, like theirs, a version of the David and Goliath contest. The film makes clear how callously the memories of many working-class women have been overridden by the official record. When these five heroines display courage and valor in finding and keeping their jobs, we cheer their personal achievement and mourn our own failure to honor their courage for all these years.

In the end, when Field tells us that even the bravest women lose the battle for access to economic opportunity, we grieve for ourselves as well as for them. But we, the children of the "Rosies' " aspirations, also absorb the meaning of their fight. The film taps the latent memory of the heroic working-class heroine in all of us, turning what might have been a pessimistic film into an oddly optimistic one. Ultimately, the failure of the "Rosies" to keep their jobs matters less than the message it provides of the tension between official memory and unfulfilled desire.

Conflicts among contemporaries and historians about the meaning of World War II for women reflect this continuing tension. Both groups fail equally in their capacity to explain how ordinary wives and mothers could so quickly have taken jobs that fundamentally contradicted seemingly enduring truths. How could so many women have sought job satisfaction in the face of generations of social signals about the primary value of reproduction, family life, and femininity? *The Life and Times of Rosie the Riveter* suggests a persuasive resolution: many women had never absorbed these messages at all. Women came into their own, these five forceful women tell us, not in the face of powerful propaganda, but in a vivid personal demonstration of its irrelevance to their daily lives. These five recall the war as a moment when the barriers erected by a gendered and racialized ideological universe temporarily fell, allowing them to seize opportunities that had long eluded them. During World War II, each savored for an instant some of the fruits of decent and well-paid jobs: security, satisfying work, material comforts, and the ability to provide for children. At the same time, the viewer is never allowed to forget the tacit protection offered to accepted cultural norms by government agency and employer policies. The result fosters an abiding skepticism. For the five "Rosies," the culture of American individualism and achievement was available only in tantalizing dreams.

The subtext of this film lies in its capacity to lay open a sense of what it means for a woman to aspire to full American citizenship. It challenges the viewer to redeem "Rosie's" loss by transcending the ideological universe that governs her. The ideological universe within which men and women operated in the middle of the twentieth century emerged from, and persistently asserted, values having to do with family and tradition, nation and patriotism. These demanded self-sacrifice, subordination, and commitment to the home as a condition of continuing participation in the democratic process. In peacetime, women's efforts to assert individual rights were antithetical to this process. Claims to fairness, equal treatment, and economic justice on the grounds of equal access to the rights of citizenship were all denied on account of

"Women workers install fixtures and assemblies to a tail fuselage section of a
B-17F bomber (the 'Flying Fortress') at the Long Beach, California, plant of
Douglas Aircraft Company. October 1942. Office of War Information." (Courtesy
of the National Archives, photo no. 800, War and Conflict Collection)

their gender. Few questioned the assumption that women's special place
in their families required them to assume secondary places in the
paid workforce.

The war caused a strange reversal: while all workers were asked to
subvert their claims to individual rights to national well-being, women
were exhorted to subordinate earlier claims to the protection of the
family to new demands of wartime production. For large numbers who
had worked for wages before the war, it provided an opportunity not only
to question traditional assumptions about women's place, but to act on
them in the name of patriotism. It allowed female workers to imagine the
possibilities of wage work and the achievements possible within an

individualist ethos of satisfying work and adequate incomes. The war thus temporarily disrupted ideological boundaries that had restricted the choices of many women for generations. The consequences were not unambivalent. This film testifies to the willingness of working men, employers, and government agencies simultaneously to entice women down the paths that provided access to jobs and to ensure that opportunity in the world of work would not diffuse commitment to traditional values. While government representatives insist in the film that no woman would be able to "walk the streets without becoming acquainted with the idea that she was needed," the same representatives describe the jobs she would do as just like those she had done at home.

But women, like the five "Rosies" in this film, chose not only to respond to the message of opportunity, but to expand on it. The result, as Belcher tells us, is often startling:

> I went to school after work for four hours so that when I got out of there, I could get a job welding. [After the war] I took my card and all my credentials and I laid my papers on the desk. He [the hiring official] said, "If you was a man, we'd hire you, but we can't hire you, you're a woman."

Field exploits experiences like this to illustrate in each of her five "Rosies" a more capacious faith in individual achievement than is typically associated with women of the war years. Each has a larger vision of justice that includes race and gender, and each demonstrates that her prewar experiences nurtured a healthy skepticism about women's traditional roles.

Indeed, Field may well have chosen her protagonists for that reason. In a subsequent interview, she recalled that the five met quite specific criteria. "We were only interested in working-class women," she said. Field indicated that she looked as well for women "forced to return to traditional jobs after the war," for some who had migrated from the rural south to the West Coast, and for women who reflected the black struggle for employment.[12] It should not come as a surprise, then, that these five women speak to an important, but by no means universal, experience. All had worked or sought paid work before the war; three of the five are African Americans (a proportion more than double the proportion of black women in the labor force at that time); all worked in war industries (where less than one-third of wage-earning women worked). Three of the five were married women during the war years, a figure that reverses that of most married women, among whom 65 percent refused to enter the labor force. Four of the five had children, but most mothers with young children entered the paid workforce only reluctantly, if at all. One guesses, then, that like many female wage workers in the 1930s, these women had lived outside normative ideology before the war began.

In contrast, the World War II "Rosies" of the propaganda clips appear as middle-class women, mostly white—sometimes past middle age—whose nurturing and family instincts join with patriotism to inspire them to sign up for the wartime workforce. "Every girl should do what she can to win this war," says one. The newsreel "Rosies" struggle to remain feminine even as they redefine its meaning. "I like it here, and it saves on clothes," says one, responding to wartime calls for frugality and sacrifice. Their skills are minimal, seemingly related to their old jobs at home: operating a metal cutter is just like cutting a dress pattern, the government narrator tells us. Their need for income is marginal. Doggedly affirming the sanctity of the traditional family, they repeat part of the "Rosie the Riveter" hit tune: "Rosie is protecting Charlie"—who is a Marine. Newsreel "Rosies" insist that they are merely doing their bit, "working only to win the war," eager to "return to their home duties after the war is won." They are mothering the men in uniform by providing them with the bullets and guns they need to do their jobs.

For Field's on-camera "Rosies," family and wage work constitute an almost seamless web; their exclusion from remunerative jobs before and after the war is remembered with angry regret. Each of these five competent women imagines herself to be a working woman. One describes herself as "a widow with a child to support." Another comments, "I had two small children." Only Weixel insists on her right to work: "I was a working woman," she tells us forthrightly. Employed at women's jobs before the war, each seized the main chance when the opportunity presented itself. As Childs says, she took a war job because "number one, I needed work; number two, I'd had bad experience in jobs before where I hadn't felt any pride in the kind of work I was doing; number three, there was a war on and the people were all enthused about helping out in every way they could." They traveled across country when necessary, leaving friends and family behind. They eagerly and rapidly learned the necessary skills. "We were going to get in on the ground floor and be welders for ever and ever," says Weixel. They temporarily overcame racial and sexual prejudice to get good jobs in war industries. Their jobs were personally satisfying and permitted them to live and support children without male support. Three of these five became leaders in their workplaces, and all five protested their rude dismissal at the end of the war.

A win-the-war mentality sustained their efforts and justified their work as a defense of the "American way of life," even as wartime restrictions sought both to limit women's gains and to circumscribe their meaning. The newsreel clips and propaganda shorts reveal how women were urged to join the workforce through appeals to patriotism. A narrator tells women that they constitute a hidden army that will provide the planes and ammunition without which servicemen cannot win the war; women in the newsreels repeat the point. One advises the audience that she is working "for the nation in its time of need." Another insists that she is only doing her duty—"What woman wouldn't?" In the official and unofficial voice of the time, the language of individualism seems to be muted. Women are told that they are working for the home, and their pictures in black-and-white tell us that their families now consist of all the men who have gone to war. "I'm an old maid. Now I've got a family of 10 million to look after," says one in rehearsed lines that ring so hollow today. Women's own desires and needs are said to be selfish and divisive. To absent oneself from work to go shopping—"the day after payday is no time to relax," the women are reminded—or to quit work when one's material desires have been fulfilled is no less than treasonous and is decried as a major contributor to the rising number of military casualties.

The memories speak a different experience: the money and the job satisfaction mattered to the five real "Rosies," and they took unequivocal pride in both despite the difficulties of doing two jobs. "Having worked for a dollar a day or ten dollars a week, it was good to be getting a hundred dollars because I had never made that much money," says one. Experience recalls how difficult that task was, while families remained a constant demand. Earning wages often required heroic efforts to preserve the home, sometimes to no avail. Childs remembers with heart-wrenching grief her inability to bring her daughter with her to California. Allen sent two daughters to boarding school because she could not keep them and work at the same time. None found really good child care. They simply coped. Even the routine requirements of housework could prove daunting. Overtime took a devastating toll on women who managed households while working at demanding jobs. "Ten hours was just too much for me," Allen recalls. "I didn't mind doing eight and an occasional nine, but ten was just too much. I just couldn't do it." And Weixel (who

During the war, the Office of War Information captioned this publicity photograph: "Secretaries, housewives, waitresses, women from all over central Florida are getting into vocational schools to learn war work. Typical are these in the Daytona Beach branch of the Volusia county vocational school. April 1942. Howard R. Hollem." (Courtesy of the National Archives, photo no. 801, War and Conflict Collection)

lived with her husband's family while he was in the military) comments on the tiring work of helping her mother-in-law, while the men of the household merely relaxed.

To sustain the image of the temporary worker, the propaganda shorts invoked the language of masculinity and femininity to describe the ways in which women workers could save on stockings, adhere to safe dress codes while looking attractive, and leave the heavy jobs to male workers. But in the memories of the real-life "Rosies," these issues appear not at all. For them, struggles against racism, for safe working conditions, and for equal pay dominate, constituting some of the film's most powerful moments.

In the bomb-casing plant where Weixel worked, female employees tried to unionize when they discovered that "we were earning far less than men who were doing the same work." The boss accepted the idea that men might be union members, but rejected women's efforts to organize. To him, Weixel remembers, "we were only good . . . for being married and having babies. That's all we were good for." Their strike revealed differential wages not only between men and women doing the same work, but between black and white women as well. "They were paid five cents less per hour than the white workers had been paid," recalls Weixel in disgust. "Talk about cheap."

All three black workers tell stories about endemic racism. Childs was refused a job as a ship's welder because black women were generally not hired for that occupation. "I thought I was well qualified," she insists. She argued her way into becoming a burner, a job that paid better. Later she intervened forcefully on behalf of a male Filipino worker who had been cruelly beaten by his foreman. Her demand that he be treated the same as other workers led the military officer in charge at the shipyard to back down and support her. Allen could not get a war industry job until she agreed to serve as a test case at the request of a union representative. She sat determinedly in a Detroit factory employment office, effectively stopping the hiring process, until managers agreed to hire black women. Later, outraged that the women's showers in the factory were available only to whites, she and other women of color led a successful union battle to desegregate the clean-up facilities. Wright encountered a series of unsafe and even mortally dangerous jobs where black women were routinely assigned and where prescribed safety equipment was not provided. She and other workers abandoned those jobs until they found safer places of work.

As the living "Rosies" learned that better qualifications and more responsibility did not necessarily lead to better pay and job prospects, they discovered the gap between the ability of men and of women to achieve the American dream. For minorities, the American dream was especially remote. The gap is particularly obvious when issues of the household are considered because none of the five women featured in this film could comfortably manage to do full-time paid work and all the household tasks as well. The failure of companies to help female employees fulfill their responsibilities to their homes becomes an additional source of distress and is interpreted as a violation of their right to good jobs.

Finally, each of the "Rosies" recalls how, after her own commitment to equality and fairness was encouraged by wartime hopes, these ideals

After a long struggle, some women of color were accepted as welders before the end of the war. The wartime caption on this photograph identifies only three of these women: " 'Welders Alivia Scott, Hattie Carpenter, and Flossie Burtos await an opportunity to weld their first piece of steel on the ship [SS *George Washington Carver*].' Kaiser Shipyards. Richmond, CA. Ca 1943. E. E. Joseph" (Courtesy of the National Archives, photo no. 252, African Americans in World War II Collection)

were subsequently rudely violated in the war's aftermath as she was quickly displaced from her job. "I thought I had several skills that were . . . very good and I wouldn't have any problem getting a job anywhere else," Wright says. Belcher has similar memories. She was "a widow woman, a lone woman. My children had to be taken care of, and I'd bought a little home. It had to be paid for. I had to get a job somewhere, somehow." Finally, she found work in a restaurant kitchen: "Hot hard work. Heavy lifting. It was a lot harder than working in the shipyard and a lot less pay." A demobilization in which 75 percent of the women wanted to keep their jobs and most were forced out of them, or pushed down into less desirable occupations, left an inevitable residue of extreme bitterness. What the propaganda shorts portray as only fair (to men returning from the armed services), inevitably appeared to many women war workers as no less than sex discrimination.

If the experience of war and the events of the postwar period placed the home on the national agenda, they also heightened women's ability to understand the limits on their own work-related aspirations. The genius of Field's film is that it captures two messages. One, provided by the narrators and other authorities in the propaganda shorts, insists that women's war jobs merely extended their roles as mothers and wives—a view that neither Mead nor Farnham and Lundberg contested. The second, provided by the women interviewed by Field, suggests how much they appreciated and valued that aspect of the war experience for the dreams it allowed. Ironically, perhaps, even the five "Rosies" only begin to suggest the challenge to the official line that was to come later. For the most part, they justify their continuing desire for good jobs after the war in terms of support for their families.

The drive for fair treatment in the workforce resonates with contemporary viewers. When Allen appeared at a film showing in 1981, she received a standing ovation, "a moving demonstration of respect," according to historian Barbara Wertheimer, and a statement of appreciation by an audience that was saying, "We understand. You paved the way for our gain. We thank you."[13] In the end, then, this is a film in which the struggle on the screen speaks to the continuing dilemma of most women's lives: the desire to function as women *and* as workers in an environment framed to deny the reality of that possibility.

The success of *The Life and Times of Rosie the Riveter* lies in the way it validates and provides comfort to the participants in an on-going struggle for gender equity. By validating the lives of ordinary working women and pitting their remembered wartime experience against official public justifications, the film suggests the value of memory in restoring that experience and affirms the usefulness of memory as a historical source. Its persuasive picture of women as courageous and earnest workforce participants, as eager as men to nurture the American culture of individualism and achievement, provokes skepticism about ideological tropes that come from outside real experience. The result vividly suggests the importance of the subjective encounter—the lived experience. The film taps the desire of today's young women for historical legitimacy, providing evidence that their own movement for gender equity is not new or newly rooted. It thus sustains a profoundly political message: what working women have gained must not be easily relinquished.

NOTES

1. Margaret Mead, "The Women in the War," in *While You Were Gone: A Report on Wartime Life in the United States,* ed. Jack Goodman (New York: Simon and Schuster, 1946), p. 286.

2. Ibid., pp. 288–89.

3. Marynia F. Farnham and Ferdinand Lundberg, *Modern Woman: The Lost Sex* (New York: Harper, 1947), pp. 363–64.

4. Ibid., pp. 355–77.

5. For example, see Alice Kessler-Harris, *Out to Work: A History of Wage Earning Women in the United States* (New York: Oxford University Press, 1982), pp. 273–99; and Sherna Berger Gluck, *Rosie the Riveter Revisited: Women, the War, and Social Change* (Boston: Twayne, 1987), pp. 1–18.

6. See Sheila Tobias and Lisa Anderson, "What Really Happened to Rosie the Riveter: Demobilization and the Female Labor Force, 1945–47," cited in Leila J. Rupp, *Mobilizing Women for War: German and American Propaganda, 1939–1945* (Princeton: Princeton University Press, 1978), p. 142n; Karen Anderson, *Wartime Women: Sex Roles, Family Relations, and the Status of Women During World War II* (Westport, Conn.: Greenwood Press, 1981); Maureen Honey, *Creating Rosie the Riveter: Class, Gender, and Propaganda During World War II* (Amherst: University of Massachusetts Press, 1984); and Robert B. Westbrook, " 'I Want a Girl, Just Like the Girl That Married Harry James': American Women and the Problem of Political Obligation in World War II," *American Quarterly* 42, no. 4 (December 1990): 587–614.

7. "Rosie the Riveter" was a popular wartime song; its alliterative title became a general term for women working in war-related industries. *The Life and Times of Rosie the Riveter* (Clarity Educational Productions), 65 minutes, color and black-and-white. Connie Field, producer/director; Cathy Zheutlin, Emiko Omori, Bonnie Friedman, and Robert Handley, cinematography; Field and Lucy Massie Phenix, editors; and Peter Adair, contributing editor. For full data, see "The Life and Times of Rosie the Riveter," *Monthly Film Bulletin* 48, no. 575 (December 1981): 248–49.

8. Connie Field, interview with Daniel Bickley, in Bickley, "Who's Who in Filmmaking: Connie Field," *Sightlines* 14 (Summer 1981): 23–25.

9. Barbara Wertheimer, "Rosie the Riveter—A Generation Later," in *The Life and Times of Rosie the Riveter: The Story of Three Million Working Women During World War II,* ed. Miriam Frank, Marilyn Ziebarth, and Field (Emeryville, Calif.: Clarity Educational Productions, 1982), p. 8. This is the companion book and study guide for the film.

10. Gerald Fraser, "Rosie's Life After the War Was Not So Rosy," *New York Times,* May 2, 1981, p. C13.

11. Ibid. See also John Coleman, "LFF XXV," *New Statesmen,* November 27, 1981, pp. 32–33; John Dowling, "Films," *Bulletin of the Atomic Scientists* 37 (October 1981): 41–42; Molly Haskell, "Six Films to Go Out of Your Way to See," *Ms.,* January 1981, p. 22; Stanley Kauffmann, "Spring Roundup," *New Republic,* May 23, 1981, p. 24; and Arthur Schlesinger, Jr., "History and the Imagination," *American Heritage,* October–November 1981, p. 92. See also my first response to the film, Alice Kessler-Harris, " 'Rosie the Riveter': Who Was She?" *Labor History* 24 (Spring 1983): 249–53. The passage of time and the emergence of new research findings have led me to modify my initial response.

12. Field interview in Bickley, "Who's Who in Filmmaking," p. 24.

13. Wertheimer, "Rosie the Riveter," p. 8.

8

Men of Bronze (U.S., 1980) and *Liberators* (U.S., 1992): Black American Soldiers in Two World Wars

CLEMENT ALEXANDER PRICE

Many years after he became one of the first of the Allied troops to enter Buchenwald concentration camp, Leon Bass, a black American, observed:

> On this day in April in 1945, with some of my comrades, I walked through the gates of a place called Buchenwald. I was totally unprepared for what I saw. Someone of 19 couldn't have been prepared, for he hasn't lived long enough. I was still trying to develop my value system. I was still trying to sort things out, and then all of a sudden, slap—right in the face—was the horror perpetrated by man against man.[1]

In the aftermath, as this poignant statement suggests, America's wars have often brought blacks and whites much closer to the complex interweaving of individual courage, cowardice, national purpose, and collective memory, and closer still to the discovery that battlefields can become symbolic of the larger struggle for racial justice in the United States.

America's major wars have been associated with such profound domestic changes in race relations and black life that they seem to overshadow the larger terrain of historical causation and change. Consider, for example, how historians have viewed the American Revolution as a catalyst for the First Emancipation of slaves in the northern states,[2] or the way black military service during the Civil War has been linked in our historical imagination to the Great Emancipation of slaves in the crumbling Confederacy.[3] Writing in 1935, W. E. B. Du Bois considered the significance of the latter:

It took in many respects a finer type of courage for the Negro to work quietly and faithfully as a slave while the world was fighting over his destiny than it did to seize a bayonet and rush mad with fury or inflamed with drink, and plunge it into the bowels of a stranger. He might plead his cause with the tongue of Frederick Douglass, and the nation listened almost unmoved. He might labor for the nation's wealth, and the nation took the results without thanks, and handed him as near nothing in return as would keep him alive. He was called a coward and a fool when he protected the women and children of his master. But when he rose and fought and killed, the whole nation with one voice proclaimed him a man and brother. Nothing else made emancipation possible in the United States. Nothing else made Negro citizenship conceivable, but the record of the Negro soldier as a fighter.[4]

The image of warfare as an arena where blacks more successfully fought for their rights than during times of peace became a historical construct as powerful in intent as it was in impact by the early twentieth century. This image helped both to shape and to distort the past during a time when black Americans, along with other Americans, were fighting wars increasingly farther from home and returning with more sophisticated views of what war can do in a protracted struggle against injustice.

For nearly two generations, historians have argued that World War I was instrumental in shaping modern black thinking, that it enabled blacks to consider the Caucasian race from a broader perspective than was possible on the South's dusky roads, and that it placed the blacks' quest for justice within the larger quest for a more sane and tolerant world order. As Du Bois was to observe about black veterans at the end of the war, "We return. We return from fighting. We return fighting. Make way for Democracy! We saved it in France, and by the Great Jehovah, we will save it in the USA, or know the reason why," which in retrospect signaled, along with other postwar rhetoric by black leaders, the beginning of the "New Negro Era."[5]

It is now generally agreed that World War II also reshaped black America's long quest for an end to racial segregation. That war unleashed discontent with racial injustice and led to a broad discussion of the nation's white-over-black social system. It brought to light the first stirring of the modern civil rights movement; gave new life to the great migration from the South; dramatized scores of local challenges to racial discrimination in employment, housing, and politics; brought state and federal agencies into the business of race relations and encouraged black Americans to consider their plight and promise within the context of a color line that extended from Japan to South Africa to Brazil to the sprawling ghettos of the northern United States.[6]

The depiction of war amid the life and times of Afro-Americans in motion pictures has followed a similar line of reasoning. Films that deal with the unique role and image of black soldiers focus on the significance of great wars as turning points in Afro-American history and as epochs in which the nation's racial injustices become all the more perceptible.[7] To an extent, these films reacted to the nation's traditional devices employed in the historical construction of blacks, specifically the stereotypical depiction of black men under arms. Ever conscious of the seductive power of the classically racist film—*The Birth of a Nation* (U.S., 1915) by D. W. Griffith—and of a subsequent generation of white filmmakers, black filmmakers have consciously sought to emphasize a more positive image of the race.[8]

Men of Bronze (U.S., 1980) and *Liberators: Fighting on Two Fronts in World War II* (U.S., 1992) are nuanced documentations and counterimages of blacks during two world wars. They challenge the stereotype that black men could not fight heroically in battle, an image strengthened by the preponderant attention given to white soldiers.

Aside from the difficulties that can arise when a group overcompensates for racial mythology, the two films, as documentations of real events, present historians with a perplexing set of problems. Do moving images of black soldiers enhance an understanding of the black experience in war, or do they, like so many written documents, reflect a circumscribed view of the race? If the historian of Afro-American life is to be wary of words written by whites during the war, what are we to make of the pictures that whites took? In short, did the camera lie? To what extent should the historian be skeptical of the current tendency of many movies about blacks in the world wars to embolden historical imagery with sentiments that have arisen only recently? Should movies be held to customary scholarly standards of accuracy? Finally, do documentaries, which form an important part of cinematic treatment of blacks during war, provide a believable look at a particular historical event, issue, or moment?

My sense of these dilemmas is shaped to a great extent by personal experience in using film to popularize black history to predominantly black audiences. In 1973, local residents, assembled by New Jersey's Newark Museum, started screening movies at an annual Newark Black Film Festival. The festival began after the Newark riots of 1967 as a sensible alternative to the tension of long, hot summers in the city. It was supported initially by the Annenburg Center at the University of Pennsylvania.

From the beginning of the series, the most popular films were documentaries that sought to revise traditional historical interpretation through image, connecting narrative, and black genre music. Such works purport to be within the domain of serious scholarship; they feature the documented facts of history juxtaposed with grainy footage of blacks at the threshold of modernism. And they support a linear story with what blacks have long respected in both their historical and modern experiences—oral testimony. The films often include a compelling narrative delivered with poetic authority by voices known to black Americans as belonging to persons of proven honesty—well-known actors such as Bill Cosby, Ossie Davis, Ruby Dee, and Denzel Washington, or Gil Noble, a New York–based black television journalist. Most of these films, including *Men of Bronze* and *Liberators,* are remarkably well done. They are moderate in tone, informed in large part by written history and extant primary source material that is presented as visual support for the narrative and the moving or still images.

Men of Bronze examines the formation and exploits of the famous 369th United States Infantry Regiment during World War I. It was directed by William Miles, whose film credits also include *A Different Drummer* (U.S., 1983), *Paul Robeson: Man of Conscience* (U.S., 1986), *Black Champions* (U.S., 1986), *James Baldwin: The Price of the Ticket* (U.S., 1989), *Black Stars in Orbit* (U.S., 1990), and, most recently, *Liberators.* By skillfully weaving together historical footage of black soldiers in battle in France with oral-history testimony of black veterans and spoken narrative, *Men of Bronze* is arguably the finest documentary on black military service. It captures the spirit of black heroism, especially in its treatment of two of the war's most outstanding fighters, Henry Johnson and Needham Roberts, who repulsed a raiding party of German troops at Bois-Hanzey in the Argonne on May 5, 1918. It provides testimony about the impact of military service by men of color throughout the African Diaspora on American blacks and features footage of the homecoming accorded returning black troops in the famous parade that took them from downtown Manhattan to enthusiastic crowds in Harlem.

More significantly, the film explores the prevailing notion at the beginning of the Great War that blacks were unsuitable for military service.

Historically, blacks had countered such perceptions through heroism and death on the battlefield, but the race had to virtually reinvent its military image in each succeeding war, including World War I.[9] For its courage and gallantry at Maison-en-Champagne, the entire 369th Regiment was awarded by the French government the Croix de Guerre, and 171 officers and enlisted men in the regiment received the Legion of Honor.

Yet, in an attempt to challenge white hegemonic history, Miles mediates history in ways that many historians who work exclusively with words would find unsatisfactory. We are presented with a portrait of black military history that actually conjures up popular notions of white courage in battle; indeed, for a skeptical scholar, the underlying message is that black men under arms acted like white men with black skins— nothing more, nothing less. In relying on the dominant culture's notions of manly courage, the documentary overlooks the possibility of black cowardice and the uncertainty that some blacks harbored over the propriety of fighting to defend a European colonial power. These are admittedly delicate issues for any race, especially difficult to explore in a film about American blacks, whose inability to rise up, fight, and kill had long seemed a negative stereotype to be rejected as simply false. But to the historian who wants to scrutinize the construction of a black heroic tradition in battle, the past seems pressed into dubious service of the present. Certainly, black men and women voiced their support for the war effort of the United States and its allies, but in *Men of Bronze,* that is the only voice we hear. The film is nuanced in ways that make it difficult to accept as an accurate reconsideration of the past. Rather, *Men of Bronze,* though a compelling documentary on a neglected chapter about the Great War, is a heroic rendering of historical footage as well as still photographs and oral-history interviews. In making its argument that blacks saw the war as a drama in which to display qualities the world needed to see, the film sheds light on a far too simple past.

Liberators: Fighting on Two Fronts in World War II, co-produced and co-directed by Nina Rosenblum and William Miles, presents a more troubling set of problems about the use of film. It was shown in the United States over the Public Broadcasting System on November 11, 1992. Not unlike what *Men of Bronze* describes for World War I, it explores racism in World War II's segregated American armed forces, black military service during that time, and the legacy of the war. It relies heavily on oral-history testimony.

In America's segregated army in World War II, two soldiers in an unidentified all-black unit train in a light tank at Montford Point Camp, North Carolina, April 1943. (National Archives, photo no. 180, African Americans in World War II Collection)

Liberators is an especially provocative film because its release coincided with, and obviously sought to address, contemporary tensions that exist between American blacks and American Jews. After more than a half-century in which the two groups had been publicly linked as a formidable alliance in the struggle for racial justice, during the waning years of the modern civil rights movement, divisions and conflicts between the two groups became the norm.[10] Black and Jewish leaders disagreed over the issues of affirmative action and quotas in employment and educational opportunities. These tensions were crystallized in the United States Supreme Court decision in *Regents of the University of California v. Allan Bakke,* and in disagreements over U.S. foreign policy in the Middle East. More recently, relations between the two groups worsened as a result of a number of highly publicized incidents, including the anti-Semitic speeches of Leonard Jeffries, a black studies professor at the City University of New York, and the killing of a rabbinical student, Yankel Rosenblum, by a mob of black youths in the 1991 riot in the Crown Heights section of Brooklyn.[11] Where blacks and Jewish Americans had once seemed cooperative, the hard reality of ethnic struggle seemingly threatened more than two generations of interracial harmony.[12]

Against this backdrop, and because it deals in part with the role that black soldiers played in rescuing Jewish survivors of the Nazi Holocaust, *Liberators* is a symbolic testament to earlier black and Jewish cooperation. Its official premiere was held on December 11, 1992, at the Apollo Theater in Harlem, where 1,200 black and Jewish patrons saw it, including the Reverend Jesse Jackson, Peggy Tishman of the Jewish Community Relations Council, and New York City Mayor David Dinkins (the first black ever to hold that office), who said that the work of reconciliation between blacks and Jews "will take more than one film and one evening," but that the screening was "the first volley in a long campaign."[13]

Liberators uses World War II footage of black soldiers, oral-history testimony of black soldiers in the 761st Tank Battalion and the 183rd Combat Engineers, plus testimony of Jewish survivors of the Holocaust. Their on-camera accounts tell the poignant story of America's racial intolerance, black heroism in battle, and the most extreme consequences of racism in the German concentration camps. Hence the documentary places the difficulties of American blacks within a far more frightening context of race relations than any previous film dealing with war. In the process, however, it replaces historical inquiry with moral drama.

In the film, the memory of black soldiers fighting overseas embraces those who benefited from their exploits—these survivors of the Holocaust. A group of black veterans is seen returning to places in France where they are reunited with those whose villages they entered as a part of the final grand assault against the German army. Black veterans Leonard Smith and E. G. McConnell walk through Buchenwald with Benjamin Bender, one of its survivors, to see and discuss what remains of the concentration camp's infamous infrastructure. *Liberators* thus joins memory with historical and contemporary footage to support a contemporary appeal for humanity and a linear story of black military heroism amid the Holocaust and American racism.

Historical inquiry often leads to the kind of rich texture found in *Liberators;* however, by ignoring standards of scholarly accuracy, the producers and directors committed a number of errors that have made *Liberators* one of the most controversial films of its genre. Soon after its

Black soldiers of the 761st Tank Battalion clean their .30–caliber machine guns and prepare their tanks in England in September 1944 before leaving to go into action in France and Germany with Patton's Third Army. (U.S. Army Signal Corps. National Archives photo 111–SC-194874).

release, the documentary was criticized for its historical inaccuracies. On closer scrutiny, a review team assembled by television station WNET in New York, which aired the film and sponsored its national release on the Public Broadcasting System, concluded that the 761st Tank Battalion and the 183rd Combat Engineers, both black units, did *not,* as stated, liberate the Buchenwald and Dachau camps in Germany. They did reach them within forty-eight hours of the U.S. Army division that actually arrived there first. In addition, the film was found to have other historical inaccuracies that revealed the danger of relying too heavily on oral testimony alone. The review team did find, however, that the 761st Tank Battalion was a part of the liberating force that entered Gunskirchen, a subcamp of Mauthausen, *Austria,* on May 4 and 5, 1945.[14] As a result of its findings, WNET refused to allow additional use of the film on public-television stations.

A far more exhaustive, carefully documented study of the film was made by Kenneth S. Stern, program specialist on anti-Semitism and extremism for the American Jewish Committee. Stern concludes that the film's essential message of black GI involvement in the liberation of survivors in concentration camps was true, as was their heroic military role in the armed forces despite many racial obstacles and the subsequent indifference accorded them in military history.[15] Yet Stern argues that the film "has serious factual flaws, well beyond what can be written off as 'artistic license.' " What was lost in the film was an opportunity to deal with the real, verifiable stories of black soldiers rescuing Jews from Dachau and Buchenwald and the liberation of Mauthausen by the 761st Tank Battalion. When asked to provide sources for historical information presented in their film, Rosenblum and Miles were unwilling or unable to do so. Moreover, as Stern argues, some of the testimony attributed to black veterans and Jewish survivors was twisted to fit an inaccurate story. He writes, "There was, tragically, a real story that could have been told to make the same point as the factually erroneous one."[16]

The factual errors of the film are found as well in an accompanying book by Lou Potter with Miles and Rosenblum, which also relies heavily on unsubstantiated oral testimony and ignores the implications of some important documentary evidence. In a map which shows that the path of the 761st Tank Battalion in March and April 1945 took it far to the north of Dachau, a note simply indicates, without substantiation, that the map "does not show the path of the numerous so-called bastard units that moved through the Munich-Dachau regions." Stern's interviews with two officers with the battalion, Charles Gates and Paul Bates, found "that there is no way any of the tanks could have been involved in the liberation of either Buchenwald or Dachau." Other members of the battalion, McConnell, Philip W. Latimer, and David J. Williams, also dispute the film's claim that the 761st liberated the two camps; the book does not address the obvious discrepancy with what some veterans remembered about their actions.[17] The book was hastily remaindered by the publisher. That decision, when considered along with the action taken by WNET to dissociate itself from the film, turned the controversy over *Liberators* into a metaphor for cinematic disaster and led many to consider anew problems in guaranteeing the authenticity of historical documentary films.

Path of the Liberators, March–April 1945. As this map makes clear, the black 761st Tank Battalion was never near Buchenwald or Dachau, Germany, despite the claims of the television documentary *Liberators* (U.S., 1992) that it had liberated those infamous concentration camps. After fighting its way through Germany, the 761st Battalion did, in fact, help in the liberation of another concentration camp, a subcamp of Mauthausen, in Austria, near Linz. The names of concentration camp sites are in capital letters. The companion book to the documentary adds an asterisk to a somewhat different map of the route of the battalion through Germany, without explaining just what the following might mean: "While this map indicates the path of the main units of the 761st, it does not show the paths of the numerous so-called bastard units that moved through the Munich–Dachau region." (Map by Bryon Weathersby and Andrea Caillouet, Division of Instructional Support and Development, Louisiana State University, 1995. Reprinted by permission)

In sum, because *Liberators* sought to cover a profoundly difficult and broad historical event with too thin a line of historical information, its basic argument that black troops were liberators is thrown into the difficult post-Holocaust struggle between memory and fact, historical interpretation and historical denial. It is true that black soldiers were among the first to enter the camps, but because of flaws in the film, their stature as liberators, and as rescuers, has needlessly been brought into question. The producers and directors seemingly ignored the inconsistencies found in the stories of some black veterans and failed to subject their testimony to other sources of information. When the controversy surrounding the inaccuracies in the film arose, they chose to defend their film as a victim of racist attempts to discredit the contributions of blacks to the Allied war effort. However, that claim, which has been made for many years by scholars of the black experience, conflicts with the intense scrutiny required of those who study the causes and consequences of the Holocaust. Factual errors in that modern tragedy invite a profound misconstruction of the history and memory of inhumanity during the war years. "The fact is," Stern writes, "there are Holocaust deniers working today with an agenda harmful for both blacks and Jews. It is the deniers who wait to pounce on any inconsistency in historical memory, and then repaint what occurred without care for detail."

The problems implicit in *Liberators* are, of course, not foreign to historians whose work is revealed only in words. There is always the temptation to draw conclusions without sufficient supporting or corroborating documentation. And the world of traditional historiography has never been immune to using memory as the basis for fact. The world of historical film documentation, though, is far more susceptible to error because it seeks not so much to render an accurate account of the past as to reintroduce us to feelings about the past. As Robert A. Rosenstone has observed:

> If short on traditional data, film does easily capture elements of life that we might wish to designate as another kind of data. Film lets us see landscapes, hear sounds, witness strong emotions as they are expressed with body and face, or view physical conflict between individuals and groups. Without denigrating the power of the written word, one can claim for each medium unique powers of representation.[18]

Films like *Men of Bronze* and *Liberators* should especially serve a larger public need for scholarly objectivity to compete with historical passion. Moving pictures do have powers that the written word does not.

Within the context of black history, these films dramatize this fact with remarkable skill, yet with remarkable flaws.

Finally, such works represent significant challenges to the way the literary construction of the past often ignores the poignancy of the black past. They provide another view of great human conflict and its aftermath; they also demonstrate the ability of film to manipulate imagery of the past for popular consumption. Historians usually see the pitfalls in taking on such a task, knowing only the fragments of the past. It must be remembered, however, that this is the nature of historical work in the first place and that, too, is the reason why films, written words, sounds, and expressed memories are all necessary for the future of the past, and must all be subjected to rigorous tests for accuracy.

NOTES

1. Leon Bass, quoted in Brewster Chamberlain and Marcia Feldman, eds., *The Liberation of the Nazi Concentration Camp, 1945: Eyewitness Accounts of the Liberators* (Washington, D.C.: United States Holocaust Memorial Council, 1987), p. 25.

2. Benjamin Quarles, *The Negro in the American Revolution* (Chapel Hill: University of North Carolina Press, 1961); Willie Lee Rose and William H. Freehling, *Slavery and Freedom* (New York: Oxford University Press, 1982), chap. 1; Arthur Zilversmit, *The First Emancipation of Slavery in the North* (Chicago: University of Chicago Press, 1967), pp. 119, 122–23, 146–47.

3. Leon F. Litwack, *Been in the Storm So Long: The Aftermath of Slavery* (New York: Random House, 1979), chap. 2; James M. McPherson, *The Negro's Civil War: How American Negroes Felt and Acted During the War for the Union* (New York: Ballantine, 1991), and *The Struggle for Equality* (Princeton: Princeton University Press, 1964), chap. 9; Willie Lee Rose, *Rehearsal for Reconstruction: The Port Royal Experiment* (New York: Random House, 1964), chap. 6.

4. W. E. B. Du Bois, *Black Reconstruction in America, 1860–1880* (New York: Russell & Russell, 1966), p. 104.

5. Quoted in John Hope Franklin and Alfred A. Moss, Jr., *From Slavery to Freedom: A History of Negro Americans*, 6th ed. (New York: Knopf, 1988), p. 310.

6. Harvard Sitkoff, *A New Deal for Blacks: The Emergence of Civil Rights as a National Issue* (New York: Oxford University Press, 1978), chap. 12; John Morton Blum, *V Was for Victory* (New York: Harcourt, Brace Jovanovich, 1976), chap. 6.

7. For example, see Paul Finkelman's review of *Glory* (U.S., 1989) a feature film that dramatized the exploits of the Massachusetts Fifty-fourth Regiment during the American Civil War, in *Journal of American History* 77 (1990): 1108.

8. Thomas Cripps, *Slow Fade to Black: The Negro in American Film, 1900–1942* (New York: Oxford University Press, 1977), chaps. 2, 3.

9. In one of the earliest general texts on Afro-American history, a pioneering black American historian wrote that "throughout this country they [the blacks] had been treated as pariahs, unprepared for the full measure of that democracy for which

Woodrow Wilson desired to fight in Europe that the world might be a decent place to live in." Moreover, "the reactionary class, . . . although ready to brand the Negroes with suspicion and to prosecute them for disloyalty, urged the government not to recruit Negroes" (Carter G. Woodson, *The Negro in Our History* [Washington, D.C.: Associated Publishers, 1945], pp. 515–16).

10. For background on Afro-American and Jewish American relations, see David Levering Lewis, "Parallels and Divergences: Assimilationist Strategies of Afro-American and Jewish Elites from 1910 to the Early 1930s," in *Bridges and Boundaries: African Americans and American Jews,* ed. Jack Salzman, with Adina Back and Gretchen Sullivan Sorin (New York: Braziller, 1992), pp. 17–35.

11. Richard Goldstein, "The New Anti-Semitism, a Geschrei," *Village Voice,* October 1, 1991, pp. 33–34, 36, 38; see also Henry Louis Gates, Jr., "Black Demagogues and Pseudo-Scholars," *New York Times,* July 20, 1992, p. A15.

12. Harold Cruse, *The Crisis of the Negro Intellectual* (New York: Morrow, 1967), pp. 476–97.

13. Ari L. Goldman, "Blacks and Jews Join Hands for a Brighter Future," *New York Times,* December 18, 1992, p. B3. In the preface of the book to accompany the film, Lou Potter followed a similar line of reasoning as to the importance of *Liberators* to contemporary black and Jewish relations: "In our rather tragic present, when black and Jewish Americans indulge in conflict that, in the final analysis, gives joy and comfort only to those racists and anti-Semites who are their common enemies, there is reason to remember a period in the not too terribly distant past. A time when those of both groups who were progressively inclined attempted with some success to collectively comprehend their horrific historical experiences" (Lou Potter, with William Miles and Nina Rosenblum, *Liberators: Fighting on Two Fronts in World War II* [New York: Harcourt Brace Jovanovich, 1992], p. xiv).

14. Thirteen/WNET Press Release, "Thirteen/WNET in New York Concludes Internal Review of Documentary *Liberators: Fighting on Two Fronts in World War II,*" September 7, 1993.

15. Kenneth S. Stern, "*Liberators:* A Background Report" (New York: American Jewish Committee, 1993), p. 1. The complete report is included in the *Historical Journal of Film, Radio and Television* 14, no. 4 (fall 1994), microfiche supplement.

16. Ibid., p. 2.

17. Ibid., p. 3.

18. Robert A. Rosenstone, "History in Images/History in Words: Reflections on the Possibility of Really Putting History onto Film," *American Historical Review* 93, no. 5 (December 1988): 1179.

9

Clement Price, *Liberators* (U.S., 1992), and Truth in History: Some Comments

DANIEL J. LEAB

The critic Roland Barthes has dealt frequently with what he calls "the pleasure of the text." Like many of his peers in our postmodern society, Barthes argues that texts of any nature often deny their own claims of authority. And he plays with what has been called the "endlessly open possibilities of language." Historians in the main respond differently to interpretations of text. They often, especially in recent years, imagine themselves defending "reality," earnestly safeguarding without assistance the threshold between fact and fiction, valorously securing a community whose inhabitants remain unconcerned about "truth."

However, as Winston Churchill—that most dogged but pragmatic of politicians and historians—pointed out years ago,

> The . . . story does not aways unfold like a mathematical calculation on the principle that two and two make four. Sometimes in life they make five or minus three; and some times the blackboard topples down in the middle of the sum and leaves the class in disorder and the pedagogue with a black eye.

Depending on your point of view, Churchill's concept may seem attractive or ludicrous.[1]

Yet in certain areas, it becomes very difficult, given the different interpretations of the text, to determine just how we should deal with it. Comments on race, class, and gender these days are often treated as though they were "pistol shots at a concert," to borrow an image from the novelist Stendahl. To what degree can we determine the truthfulness of competing versions of historic truth when we think of testing the impact of motion pictures in "the marketplace of ideas"? Clement Alexander Price, in the preceding chapter, deals with aspects of that commerce in the marketplace. In so doing, especially as regards *Liberators*, he, unlike Barthes, is not really willing to challenge the text.

Obviously each viewer of a film has his or her own version of *the* Truth. In the marketplace of ideas, therefore, as with other distinctions, there is a conflict between truth and objectivity, between those denying the authority of perceived reality and those defending "objectivity." Proponents of each set forth various definitions. Objectivity, like truth, has many self-serving definitions. Often we strive for what we claim is "objectivity," but actually do combat for our version of "reality," of truth. Supposedly, the best and cleanest test of a truth is for it to win out in the marketplace of ideas. Accordingly, would-be ideological entrepreneurs bring their products into this marketplace, expecting to prevail.

The historian and television producer Andie Tucher in her recent exploration of the origins of the "penny press" in early-nineteenth-century New York City has laid out one of the best treatments of the tensions between objectivity and truth, about what happens if a contender in the marketplace argues and loses, but does *not* accept defeat. As she points out in her book (based on her dissertation which won the 1991 Nevins Prize), there are people "so fiercely determined to rewrite historical or social reality that they persist even in the face of overwhelming evidence to the contrary."[2] In effect, such people argue that if "my truth" is not accepted "in the marketplace," that does *not* mean it is wrong. A pertinent contemporary example of that attitude is the brouhaha in New York in the early 1990s about the alleged sexual attacks on African-American teenager Tawana Brawley. Price intelligently elaborates on the question of "truth" in his essay, strongly arguing that for better or worse every community makes its own truth. That "truth" is what may well reign in a given marketplace, especially when a text becomes what media commentator Bill Moyers defines as "a fearful means for a zealous few to manipulate the minds of millions."[3]

Men of Bronze (U.S., 1980) and *Liberators* (U.S., 1992), for all their strengths, exemplify several problematic attributes. The two films are well made, technically proficient, powerful, quite moving, and visually interesting, but they are also distorted and not wholly accurate in detail. Price is right on the mark in pointing out that the filmmakers, in reclaiming some often overlooked chapters of African-American history dealing with blacks' service in the U.S. armed forces, have mustered the past "into [a] dubious service of the present."

In dealing with these two films, Price raises a host of interesting and valid questions. His answers are reasonable, moderate, and informed. He deals rationally with some very emotional issues. His treatment of the problems raised by *Men of Bronze* is exemplary. He sounds just the proper note in balancing its splendid depiction of black military service in America's armed forces during World War I with its mythic challenges to traditional stereotypes then and now. As an African American, Price, in my opinion, is admirably and remarkably restrained in his comments. Racist attitudes in World War I America led a former chief of staff of the U.S. Army to deny officer training to blacks because he did not want as officers, in his words, the kind of people "with whom our descendants cannot intermarry without producing a breed of mongrels. . . ."[4]

The nuances that Price so aptly touches on have (as he indicates) motivated black filmmaking from its earliest days. Already in 1916, taking its story from the headlines of the day, a pioneer black production company made "a thrilling picturization of the late Carrizal, Mexico[,] battle between the fighting" black troopers of the U.S. Tenth Cavalary and "the Carranzistas soldiers": *The Trooper of Troop K* (U.S., 1916) celebrated the heroism of the African-American cavalrymen participating in General John Pershing's punitive expedition into Mexico in futile pursuit of Francisco "Pancho" Villa.[5] The Lincoln Motion Picture Company's exaggerated treatment of a black trooper's heroism in a skirmish at Carrizal is echoed by *Men of Bronze,* which, as Price convincingly argues, "overcompensates for racial mythology" belittling black troops. Regardless of such excesses, director William Miles, as Price remarks, scored an impressive triumph with this film.

Liberators, despite its many virtues in emotionally memorializing the achievements of two black units, the 183rd Combat Engineers and the 761st Tank Battalion, during World War II, became, as Price puts it, "one of the most controversial films of its genre." The picture's emphasis and clear distortion, in the words of historian Lee Finkle (an expert on black protest during World War II), "refocused public attention from the contributions of black troops during World War II to the historical accuracy of the documentary."[6] The film accurately describes the troops training in a segregated America, the suffering and abuse they endured from unceasing discrimination, and their combat experiences. The strongest and ultimately most controversial part of the film focuses on the combat experiences of the men in the 761st Battalion.

Price rightly calls *Liberators* a "cinematic disaster." Because talented professionals such as Miles and his co-producers went so awry, it is worth looking more closely than Price does at aspects of the film and some of the response to it. *Liberators* was first broadcast on November 11, 1992, on PBS as part of the highly touted, award-winning series *The American Experience*, which stemmed from Boston's WGBH-TV, a source of much PBS programming.

Even before its initial airing, questions had been raised about the film's contention that in April 1945 black soldiers had helped liberate the infamous Nazi concentration camps at Dachau and Buchenwald. At no point does the film actually state that the 761st Tank Battalion was at these two *Konzentrationslager,* but the implication is clear: we see newsreel footage that includes the word "Dachau"; then two veterans of the battalion appear on screen recounting their liberation of a concentration camp and their first sight of skeletal survivors. If the veterans never mention Dachau, the filmmakers' intent is evident.

The controversy about this part of the film was fueled by charges from the American Jewish Committee, which became increasingly bitter, especially after an article entitled "The Exaggerators" appeared in the February 1993 issue of the *New Republic.*[7] That month, as WNET later pointed out, it "and The American Experience formally withdrew the film from U.S. broadcast distribution" subject to the findings of a review team that would examine the accuracy of the film's claims about black troops liberating the concentration camps.[8] The review team was led by Morton Silverstein, an Emmy Award–winning documentary filmmaker, and included Diane Wilson, a researcher who had worked for NBC News, and Nancy Ramsey, a writer whose work had appeared in *Fortune* and the *New Yorker.*

In September, the review team reported, according to a WNET press release, that "the comprehensive review process . . . has confirmed allegations that some portions of the film contain factual inaccuracies."[9] The suspension of the program became permanent, in the words of the release, "until the documentary is corrected." WNET also asked the makers of the film to remove the name of WNET (which had co-produced the film) because it did not meet the station's "standards of accuracy."[10]

My attempts to obtain copies of the findings of the review team were not successful. All I ever received from WNET, apart from a press release, was a two-page form letter from Harry Chancey, Jr., then vice president and director of program services. The all-purpose, computer-generated missive began: "When Thirteen/WNET withdrew the documentary *Liberators* . . . in February, we promised you and the viewing public a comprehensive review to evaluate allegations that portions of the film were inaccurate." After admitting to "some egregious errors," the letter concluded with thanks for "your interest in Thirteen/WNET's programs. We hope that we have been responsive to your concerns." The report was not forthcoming.[11]

Why WNET responded as it did between the initial airing of *Liberators* and the response to my inquiry may be gleaned from *New York* magazine's tag line to its story on the film: "How presumably good intentions turned a poignant World War II documentary into a fantasy of black--Jewish healing?"[12] Included in *New York*'s article was the claim by E. G. McConnell, a veteran of the 761st Tank Battalion, that what he told the filmmakers was not shown. *New York* strongly intimated that the city's emotion-charged ethnic politics had played a substantial role in the initial reception of *Liberators*.

The magazine alluded to a special screening at Harlem's Apollo Theater, at which David Dinkins, the city's first African-American mayor, who rightly expected a tough reelection campaign (he subsequently lost his bid for a second term), spoke eloquently about the film. Dinkins quoted Jewish philosophers among others. According to the *New York Times*, "an audience of 1200 blacks and Jews were moved to tears as they watched black soldiers and concentration-camp survivors recounting their shared experiences." The newspaper reported that "many hugged and passionately agreed that the screening had provided a rare powerful moment—a catharsis in the sometimes tense relations between blacks and Jews in New York City."[13] According to the *New York Post*, Holocaust survivor Elie Wiesel said that he "himself had been freed from Buchenwald by black GI's."[14]

In September 1993, after the appearance of the WNET report, with its unhappy conclusions, the *Post* found Wiesel unavailable for comment. But Mayor Dinkin's press secretary, Lee Jones, vigorously defended *Liberators*. According to the *Post*, Jones had said that "African-American soldiers played an important role in the liberation of the concentration camps, and that basic thesis of the film remains well-established."[15] True enough, the 761st Battalion did liberate some less notorious camps. But the filmmakers opted instead for the name recognition of Dachau and did not discuss the other camps.

In any event, in the marketplace of ideas there remained many who continued to accept the film's version of the truth. Miles and co-producer Nina Rosenblum stood by their work, according to the *New York Times*. They condemned WNET's "censorship" in withdrawing the film; an angry Rosenblum earlier had characterized the film's critics as "racist" and "revisionists."[16] The latter term would seem to be an exaggeration; it describes those aptly characterized by historian Michael Marcus as "malevolent cranks who claim that the Holocaust never happened."[17] To question the veracity of the film is not to deny the Holocaust.

Price's comments on *Liberators* and its impact are reasoned and unemotional. He is careful to present in detail the various critiques that have been made, especially the one by the American Jewish Committee. He enumerates with precision the reverberations that historical inaccuracy can have. Overall, his treatment of a difficult subject is sensible and sensitive. But I expected more direct commentary from Price, whose capacity for incisive and sharp commentary is highly visible in his many other publications.

His reference to "the difficult post-Holocaust struggle between memory and fact, historical interpretation and historical denial" is worrisome. The construction of this sentence equates memory with historical interpretation and fact with historical denial, equations that surely do not reflect Price's views. He is neither a revisionist nor a Holocaust denier. But as Holocaust specialist Deborah Lipstadt puts it, "future generations will not hear the story from people who can say 'this is what happened to me. . . .' For them it will be part of the distant past, and consequently, more susceptible to revision and denial."[18] When it comes to the Holocaust, denial of any kind is an obscenity, and even to consider it is heinous and sinful.

Controversy about *Liberators* continues to fuel debate. This debate extends to a book derived from the film, put together by Lou Potter with the assistance of Miles and Rosenblum.[19] The book version of *Liberators* has been remaindered; each copy contains a card that states, "It is now clear that certain facts are in dispute in *Liberators*, for which Harcourt Brace and Company must take at least partial responsibility and which we deeply regret."[20] How many people will see this card is open to conjecture: it is only laid in, and a random sampling of copies in bookstores shows that the card is often missing.

Subsequently 761st veteran E. G. McConnell, a central character in the film, sued the publisher and WNET as well as Miles and Rosenblum, with whom he had fallen into a war of words as a result of what he called their twisting of the unit's history in order to make the film "more politically pleasing."[21] His multimillion-dollar lawsuit claimed that they defamed him, injured his reputation, used his photographs and other materials without permission, and fraudulantly enticed him.

Those sued strongly contested the charges. Miles and Rosenblum released a statment signed by six black veterans and six concentration camp survivors (featured in *Liberators*) which said that the film was factual and truthful. The litigation will not reach settlement overnight. These twelve people and the makers of *Liberators* have a vision of the world that has survived some strenuous critiques of their version of the truth. That version can inspire charged public debate. But, as historian Andie Tucher points out, "a process" instead of "a product" becomes the focal point.[22]

Historian A. J. P. Taylor once charged that "history is the great propagator of doubt."[23] It raises skepticism. How is one to deal with skepticism in the marketplace of ideas? How does one dispel doubt? The literary critic Paul Fussell maintains that "understanding the past requires pretending that you don't know the present."[24] Film scholar Anton Kaes, analyzing these issues as applied to the moving image and history, argues that the past *cannot* be reexperienced but only reconstructed; to him, that history is "a closeout sale of new and old public myths."[25]

Shared understanding is what we hope for, what we strive for. What we get is a tacit understanding of these myths by a few who continue to insist on their version of the truth, no matter what the decision in the marketplace of ideas. In a culture such as ours, which, as Hilton Kramer points out, "every day grows more amnesiac about its recent past,"[26] the films dealt with by Price may revise the historical record and may even bring that necessary doubt of which Taylor spoke, but will probably have a difficult time maintaining their version of the truth in view of the opposition they have engendered. Price presciently recognizes that.

The myths that Kaes refers to are constantly in play. *Liberators,* whatever its original impact, is for now off the air and may be the subject of litigation for some time. But we have seen these films. And as the art critic John Berger argues in a somewhat different context, seeing comes before words.[27] In the seventeenth century, when men, women, and children sincerely believed in hell (where, as New England Puritan poet and clergyman Michael Wigglesworth put it, "fire and brimstone flameth"), the vision of fire meant something very different ("to dwell in endless misery") from what it does today—for example, in California's hills or an urban ghetto.

We explain the world with words—even on film (*vide* the oral histories of the black veterans in the films dealt with by Price). The relationship between what we see and what we say is never settled. The fault may be in the metaphor itself. Instead of retailing truth, as in these films, should we not instead rediscover? Whether on film, in print, or through "virtual reality," great philosophical questions can be posed, but relatively few of them can be satisfactorily answered unless we change our approach to the text, and to the truth, whatever it may be.

NOTES

Daniel J. Leab's commentary is based on Clement Price's original paper and revised article in the October 1994 issue of the *Historical Journal of Film, Radio and Television*. [Eds.]

1. Winston Churchill, quoted in Colin Bingham, ed., *Men and Affairs* (Sydney: Currawong, 1967), p. 239.

2. Andie Tucher, *Froth and Scum: Truth, Beauty, Goodness and the Ax Murder in America's First Mass Medium* (Chapel Hill: University of North Carolina Press, 1994), p. 207.

3. Bill Moyers, "Keynote Address" (Address delivered at the opening ceremonies of the National Jewish Archive of Broadcasting, The Jewish Museum, New York, March 27, 1984 [copy in author's possession]).

4. General Leonard Wood, quoted in David M. Kennedy, *Over Here: The First World War and American Society* (New York: Oxford University Press, 1980), p. 161.

5. Advertising poster, depicted in Daniel J. Leab, *From Sambo to Superspade: The Black Motion Picture Experience* (Boston: Houghton Mifflin, 1975), p. 58.

6. Lee Finkle, review of *Liberators*, *Journal of American History* 80, no. 4 (December 1993): 1192.

7. Jeffrey Goldberg, "The Exaggerators," *New Republic*, February 8, 1993, pp. 13–14. The American Jewish Committee report was prepared by one of its program specialists: Kenneth S. Stern, "Liberators: A Background Report," the American Jewish Committee, New York (copy in author's possession). It is available in microfiche format as a supplement to the *Historical Journal of Film, Radio and Television*, 14, no. 4 (Fall 1994) inside the back cover. According to Brandeis professor Thomas Doherty, perhaps the best single critique of the historical lapses in *Liberators* is a fourteen-page letter dated January 24, 1993, by attorney Gail Frey Bordon to the *Washington Post* that is on file at the U.S. Army Center of Military History, Washington, D.C.

8. WNET/WNET Press Release, "Thirteen/WNET in New York Concludes Internal Review of Documentary *Liberators: Fighting on Two Fronts in World War II*," September 7, 1993, p. 3 (copy in author's possession).

9. Ibid., p. 1. The review drew on a wide variety of archival sources whose purpose was to record, gather, and interpret material dealing with the Holocaust, the military

history of World War II, and the liberation of concentration camps. Thus the review drew on files that included the units' contemporaneous "morning reports" and "after action reports," which charted the units' whereabouts in April 1945.

10. Ibid., p. 4. For the producers of *The American Experience, Liberators* served as an unhappy benchmark. Two years later, when a program on President Franklin D. Roosevelt and the Holocaust seemed likely to cause controversy, the producers asked various specialists in twentieth-century American history to preview the film. One, Columbia University professor Alan Brinkley, in commenting on the FDR program, asserted that "this is not *Liberators* . . . it does not contain outright falsities" (Karen Everhart Bedford, "FDR Defenders Enlist TV Critics to Refute Holocaust Film," *Current,* May 9, 1994, p. 7).

11. Harry Chancey, Jr., to Daniel J. Leab, October 12, 1993 (in author's possession).

12. Stephan J. Dubner, "Massaging History," *New York,* March 8, 1993, p. 47.

13. Ari L. Goldman, "Blacks and Jews Join Hands for a Brighter Future," *New York Times,* December 18, 1992, pp. B1, B3.

14. Mel Juffe, "Ch. 13: 'Liberators' Flawed," *New York Post,* September 8, 1993, p. 7.

15. Ibid.

16. Joseph B. Treaster, "WNET Inquiry Finds No Proof Black Unit Freed Two Nazi Camps," *New York Times,* September 8, 1993, pp. B1, B3; Goldberg, "Exaggerators," p. 14.

17. Michael R. Marcus, *The Holocaust in History* (London: Penguin Books, 1986), p. xiv. It is important to understand, as a recent study well puts it, that "it is widely accepted that the perpetrators of the Holocaust . . . eventually reached the point that they decided to intentionally and calculatingly exterminate the Jews and that such extermination was largely an end in itself" (Eric Markusen and David Kopf, *The Holocaust and Strategic Bombing: Genocide and Total War in the 20th Century* [Boulder, Colo.: Westview Press, 1995], p. xii).

18. Deborah Lipstadt, *Denying the Holocaust: The Growing Assault on Truth and Memory* (New York: Free Press, 1993), p. 28.

19. Lou Potter, with Nina Rosenblum and William Miles, *Liberators: Fighting on Two Fronts in World War II* (New York: Harcourt Brace Jovanovich, 1992).

20. Insert card in author's possession. Initially the publisher had taken a much less responsive approach and had announced that it "had no plans to withdraw the book and will not attempt to add errata sheets to unshipped copies" (insert card [in author's possession]). See Calvin Reid, "*Liberators* Found Inaccurate: Harcourt Will Not Recall Book," *Publisher's Weekly,* September 13, 1993, p. 14.

21. Dubner, "Massaging History," p. 48.

22. Andie Tucher, conversation with author, October 23, 1994; see also Tucher, *Froth and Scum,* p. 204.

23. A. J. P. Taylor, quoted in a review of Adam Sismen's biography of Taylor in *The Economist,* February 19, 1994, p. 103.

24. Paul Fussell, *Thank God for the Atom Bomb and Other Essays* (New York: Summit Books, 1988), p. 24.

25. Anton Kaes, *From "Hitler" to "Heimat": The Return of History as Film* (Cambridge, Mass.: Harvard University Press, 1989), p. 196.

26. Hilton Kramer, "Notes and Comments," *New Criterion,* September 1993, p. 2.

27. John Berger, *About Looking* (New York: Pantheon, 1980), p. 175.

Conclusion

JOHN WHITECLAY CHAMBERS II

DAVID CULBERT

"Like writing history with lightning" is how President Woodrow Wilson allegedly described *The Birth of a Nation* (U.S., 1915), the silent-film epic about the U.S. Civil War and Reconstruction produced by D. W. Griffith.[1] The powerful ability of film to bring history—especially war history—to life for audiences has only increased since then, aided by technological improvements, such as sound and color, and enhanced by connections with moving images from old movie newsreels and recent television news programs.

The immediacy and apparent truth of the visual image and film's ostensible ability to propel viewers back into the past confer a sense of veracity on the most powerful historical motion pictures. But to what degree does history written with "lightning" represent the "reality" of the past?[2] To what extent is visual history an oversimplification, even a distortion, of the past?

Griffith realized that the image of war projected on the big screen was more exciting than the real thing. "Viewed as drama," he concluded, "the war is in some ways disappointing." It was the reality of World War I's trench warfare that he could not conceptualize on film: "The front lines were lacking in visual impact. Everyone is hidden away in ditches. As you look out over No Man's Land, there is literally nothing that meets the eye but an aching desolation of nothingness. . . . It is too colossal to be dramatic."[3] The reality of the western front—the long stretches of waiting and monotonous routine punctuated by periodic, plotless chaos as scattered figures darted across broken ground—was also true of World War II. Indeed, of almost any modern war.

A larger cultural function of films about war places the confused and bloody horror of modern warfare within a comprehensible and managable pattern. Feature films focus on the surface of events, providing engaging characterizations and a compelling plot, often including a love story. They provide a story with a beginning, a middle, and an end. All of this offers coherence and meaning to viewers. So in addition to the stimulating entertainment function of such motion pictures, cumulatively there may be a deeper purpose: making sense of war and its organized, if often random, violence.[4]

Narrative is, after all, a major device in real life as in fiction for organizing and interpreting disparate events, from the life of a single individual to the course of an entire war. In the West, the dominant narrative of World War I has become one of progression from idealism to disillusionment, for both victors and vanquished. If World War II has as yet no commonly agreed-on narrative, it certainly possesses a clear ideological meaning: the initial triumph and eventual destruction of fascism. This is a sense of purpose that continues to inform national histories of the war, including importantly the national history of Germany. As literary critic and memoirist Samuel Hynes has observed, World War II "was a 'good war,' or at least a just and necessary one. Young men went to war believing that, and however terrible their experiences, they returned still believing."[5]

If the carefully organized moving images of warfare in motion pictures are often more comprehensible and sometimes more exciting than war itself, and if careful photography and editing produce a directed action-oriented view of war, then particularly in the age of cinema and television, to what extent can filmic portrayals of the past offer a new "reality" of history? To what extent have the visual media become an institutional vehicle for interpreting national history for and shaping historical consciousness of the mass public in modern nations? The essays in this book raise important issues about manipulation of past events for a variety of present purposes. In this context, the authors explore the relationship of film and history, and the relationship of filmmakers' use of history to history, particularly in that most photographed of conflicts—World War II.

The most significant historical films and videos become what German film historian Anton Kaes calls "discursive events."[6] They stimulate discussion by taking positions in public debates about controversial events in the nation's past—often the recent past. The result is a dynamic interplay among fact, fiction, and memory, blurring the lines separating past from present.

Clearly, Milestone's *All Quiet on the Western Front* (U.S., 1930) is a significant historical film, prodding and engaging public views all over the world about World War I, and modern war in general. Tarkovskii's *Ivan's Childhood* (USSR, 1962), for another example, challenged official views of the Great Patriotic War during a thaw in the Soviet Union in the early 1960s. To take yet another example, the NBC television docudrama *Holocaust* (U.S., 1978) had a dramatic impact not only on its American audience but also on that in West Germany the next year. In 1979, at least one part of the eight-hour series was watched by 20 million German viewers.[7] Despite accusations of "trivialization" of the Holocaust, this American docudrama opened discussion among Germans of their own war guilt to an extent not seen since the end of the war.[8]

But most historical films fail to engage the mass public. Even the few that seek to arouse debate often fall short. Warren Beatty's *Reds* (U.S., 1981) is one example. It sought fruitlessly, at the beginning of the Reagan era, to recapture the hopes and idealism of liberal American reaction to the Russian Revolution of 1917. Viewers liked *Reds;* it made a handsome profit. Scholars debated its historical accuracy. But in the end, the picture failed to encourage public discussion about revolutionary idealism or about potential parallels between an idealistic communism of 1917 and the possibility that this legacy might suggest a less-threatening Soviet Union for the 1980s.[9]

Ken Burns's documentary *The Civil War* (U.S., 1990) is the most success-ful series about history ever to be shown on the Public Broadcasting System. But in spite of its powerful imagery and emotional evocation and its enormous audience, the series has been faulted for failing adequately to address the role of racism as a cause and a legacy of the U.S. Civil War. To historian Bruce Cumings,

> Burns's *Civil War* is a deeply conservative film, pitching a syrupy (if often eloquent) "meaning" to an audience . . . too complacent and fearful of being disturbed to want controversy. . . . It has little to do with the debates, argu-ments, contested texts, and ongoing tensions through which the real history of the Civil War retains its life and vitality.[10]

If few historical films stimulate public involvement in major historical debates, the "reading" of the ones analyzed in this book can help explicate numerous ways in which the depiction of the past has been socially constructed, something also true for books, with their competing versions of the past. Students of films that portray the past must analyze the historical context of the work itself. The investigator asks: Who created this artifact? When? Where? Why? Filmic interpretations of the past have to be placed both in the circumstances in which they were produced and in the ongoing debate over the nature and meaning of the events they portray. In the case of historical films, there are, therefore, two contexts: that in which the motion picture was made and that which it portrays. And, of course, audiences add their own cultural context, which can vary significantly as to time and place.[11]

Such films generate their sense and feeling of realism and authenticity through the accuracy of their visual detail. The sets, props, and costumes—the recycling of certain already familiar poses or scenes from newsreels or other informational media—provide reassurance as to the true-to-life quality of the film. Emphasis on petty detail—the authenticity of weapons, uniforms, helmets, insignia—seemingly inspires confidence in the historical accuracy of the entire product. But directors are often willing, for dramatic purposes, to conflate time and space and to establish a fictive history. Dialogue is created that never occurred. Characters who never met are brought together in the same room; they explain themselves in words conjured up by imaginative writers. Thus is fantasy wrapped in fact, and the difference for many—perhaps most—viewers is difficult to distinguish.

The emphasis on visual spectacle and individual drama exemplifies one of the greatest weaknesses of historical feature films—their apparent inability to examine complex causation. Written history deals with social change over time and the manifold causes for such change; it is much more difficult for historical motion pictures, especially feature films, to deal with historical trends or analytical phenomena. Large-scale social forces—war, revolution, famine, economic collapse—are portrayed mainly as the background for individuals representing a particular class, race, ethnic group, or nation, or personifying various social groups: democrats, fascists, trade unionists, industrialists, pacifists, militarists, or aristocrats. Occasionally, causation is presented briefly through the conversation and explanations of some of the characters. For example, some explanations for the cause of World War I—manufacturers' profits, rulers' pride, and military officers' desire for promotions—are discussed briefly by the soldiers in *All Quiet on the Western Front*. But the result is often simply visual stereotyping and cliché. Class structure turns out to be only aristocratic bearing, or the wearing of a riding habit or evening clothes, or the use of a monocle. The complexities of international relations elude the camera.

In *The Longest Day* (U.S., 1962), an account of the Allied invasion across the English Channel in World War II, there is not one word about causation. The Germans apparently lack understanding as to why they should resist. Allied victory is inevitable, one is tempted to say, because the Anglo-Americans have so many more Hollywood celebrities in leading roles. The day of the invasion, June 6, 1944, comes from nowhere, and the film ends with no information about the probable result of the Allied landings. A motion picture with entertainment values is undoubtedly a poor vehicle for lengthy analyses of causes and consequences, but it is Hollywood's conventions, not any inherent restriction imposed by entertainment values, that admit of nothing before or after June 6, 1944, in a film whose entire meaning turns on what happened before and after that single, momentous day.

Some filmmakers have tried to go beyond the conventions of effective Hollywood-style entertainment in addressing historical subjects. Film historian Robert A. Rosenstone argues that in the past quarter-century, a "new history film" genre has emerged as filmmakers around the world seek to probe visually the burden of the past. Such films differ in form and content from traditional historical motion pictures, which include costume dramas, dramatic re-creations, and television documentaries combining newsreel footage and interviews with participants and historians.

"New history films" often attack dominant views of the past and sometimes reject established aesthetic conventions by creating new forms for portraying and interpreting history. In so doing, they have abandoned traditional ideas of "realism" for other methods of presentation, particularly those that blur the presumptive distinction between documentary and dramatic films and that force the viewer to see that filmic history is a social construction. Few of the "new history films" have been financial successes, though they have directly confronted issues of national concern. Some examples cited by Rosenstone include *Hiroshima Mon Amour* (France–Japan, 1959), *Hitler: A Film from Germany* (Germany, 1978), *Night of the Shooting Stars* (Italy, 1982), *The Home and the World* (India, 1984), and *Repentance* (USSR, 1987). Such works invite an emotional (and a moral) response: revulsion against Nazism, hatred of colonialism's trauma, or abhorence of nuclear holocaust. Openly partisan, their aim, Rosenstone asserts, is "less to entertain an audience or make profits than to understand the legacy of the past."[12] The same is true for the rejection of Hollywood conventions by the "New German Cinema" of the 1970s in alternative films, including *Hitler, a Film from Germany* as well as *The Patriot* (Germany, 1979) and *Germany, Pale Mother* (Germany, 1980), each assessed by film scholar Anton Kaes in his fine analysis *From "Hitler" to "Heimat."*[13] Despite the methodological innovations in these films, it remains unclear how much such an alternative version of visual history will supplement more traditional genres.

The historical documentary film, frequently of more interest to scholars, appears at first glance to have greater authenticity than fictional feature films, since it is based at least in part on actuality footage from the past that it purports to document. But the reality depicted, like the past itself, is more complex and more ambiguous. John Grierson, one of England's great propagandists in the 1930s, called documentary film "the creative treatment of actuality."[14] While appearing to capture that which is seemingly real, documentaries include selected images, use camera angles that omit a larger reality, and edit and order images in such a way as to create a point of view. That point of view may be simply an interpretation or, if more tendentious, may be propaganda.[15]

It is hard to make specific claims for a greater degree of objective truth presumably found in documentary works as opposed to the presumptive nontruth found in fiction films. This applies particularly to historical feature films with specific messages—the very type discussed most frequently in this book. Indeed, one film historian who specializes in documentaries, Bill Nichols, says,

> Documentaries show us situations and events that are recognizably part of a realm of shared experience: the historical world as we know and encounter it, or as we believe others to encounter it. Utilizing the capacities of sound recording and cinematography to reproduce the physical appearance of things, documentary film contributes to the formation of popular memory. It proposes perspectives on and interpretations of historic issues, processes, and events.[16]

This sounds good, but on reflection it does not explain a greater inherent truthfulness in the documentary. For historians, it is impossible to insist on the greater historical validity of documentary as opposed to feature films. Both offer social constructs of reality.

What, then, is the proper relationship between filmmakers and historians in the filmic process of portraying and interpreting the past?[17] Despite attempts to define it, such a relationship has never been codified. Traditionally, to the extent that producers of war films—or antiwar films—contacted experts as consultants, these were military officers whose expertise was sought regarding uniforms, weapons, training, and battlefield tactics. Only in relatively recent times, and particularly with the prodding of public funding agencies such as the National Endowment for the Humanities, have producers begun to listen to professional historians about larger questions of historical accuracy. Effective collaboration requires that scholars be empathetic to visual demands of the filmmaker, and that the filmmaker be sensitive to the complexity of historical sources and events. Sometimes advice is simply ignored. Or a film can end up unlike what the adviser expected. For example, film historian Jay Leyda was embarrassed to have his name appear as a technical adviser for *Mission to Moscow* (U.S., 1943) when the final version wound up filled with propaganda in support of the Stalinist regime in Russia, America's World War II ally.[18]

Sometimes the failure of historical filmmakers to seek advice from scholars can prove disastrous. *Liberators* (U.S., 1992), a documentary television program about African-American soldiers who liberated a concentration camp in World War II, has as its central thesis a premise that is demonstrably false. The producers picked the wrong camp: the black American unit had *not* been among the liberators of the infamous concentration camp at Dachau, Germany; rather, it had liberated a lesser-known camp at Mauthausen, Austria. The filmmakers had failed to use as a consultant Robert Abzug, a historian whose *Inside the Vicious Heart: Americans and the Liberation of Nazi Concentration Camps* made him the obvious authority on the subject, and who would have been able to suggest appropriate military archival sources.[19]

The experience of Bruce Cumings, one of the leading scholars of the Korean War, as a consultant for a WGBH documentary series entitled *Korea: The Unknown War* (U.S., 1991), demonstrates how difficult such a relationship can be.[20] Cumings was so disenchanted with the process, in which his expertise and strongly expressed opinions were ignored, that he wrote a bitter attack against those who differed with him. In his book *War and Television*, Cumings rejects the argument of Boston's WGBH that he was political and the TV producers were unbiased. He simply dismisses the use of on-camera interviews of aging witnesses or participants, asserting:

> I had no trust in individual memory—which was usually a mix of badly
> remembered event, politically determined context, and contemporary de-
> sire to say the proper thing, all of it overlaid with wish fulfillment. . . . [W]e
> have been led to think that the camera's eye is better than the mind's
> eye. . . . [T]he archival photo, film, or document interacts with the repository
> of the mind's eye: memory.[21]

Effective collaboration between historical consultants and filmmakers cannot exist without some accommodation by both parties, albeit within the canons of historical scholarship. The role of the consultants in a documentary about Leni Riefenstahl reveals how this can happen. Ray Mueller's *Die Macht der Bilder* (The Power of Images) (Germany, 1992) is a three-hour documentary about the woman who directed *Triumph of the Will* (Germany, 1935), an apotheosis of Hitler that is one of the most powerful documentary films ever made. As *The Wonderful Horrible Life of Leni Riefenstahl* (an English title insisted on by Riefenstahl herself), Mueller's film has been shown on television and in movie theaters in Britain, Germany, and the United States.

The three consultants—one from Germany, one from England, and one from the United States—were satisfied with the resulting film, for they never expected to counterbalance fully the lifetime of evasions that make up Riefenstahl's half-century career. Nor did Mueller, the director. The consultants were pleased that Mueller adopted their research strategy of contrasting Riefenstahl's forceful on-camera evasions and retorts—at one point, she even physically threatened the diminutive director—with numerous voiceover excerpts from the published diaries of Nazi Propaganda Minister Joseph Goebbels. These directly contradict Riefenstahl's claim after World War II that Goebbels and the Nazi hierarchy had not been her sponsors but instead had done virtually everything possible to prevent her from making her film of the Nazi Party rally in Nuremberg.

Neither the director nor the producer of the 1992 documentary were clear initially as to what use might be made of historical consultants, who had to answer questions of fact and to suggest overlooked sources. Riefenstahl was delighted with the selection of the prominent English film historian Kevin Brownlow, since he had once published an ardent defense of her political naiveté. However, she told the director and producer that she could not stand the writings of the German consultant. And as for the American consultant, she added: "I do not trust him either." Riefenstahl provided archival footage, assented to on-camera interviews, and agreed not to try to control the finished product. Nevertheless, the producer spent numerous days negotiating with her as to what might or might not be included in the film. The consultants were not offended when their own on-camera interviews, filmed in Munich, ended up on the cutting-room floor. They screened the rough cut, but did not expect to control absolutely the final content of the release print. They were satisfied because they believed that the film effectively exposed Riefenstahl's evasions about her role in Hitler's Germany.[22]

On some matters, there is unanimity between historical consultants and filmmakers. They agree about the danger of recycling visual images. Because of the historical power of filmic images, Anton Kaes argues, "the further the past recedes, the closer it becomes."[23] The photographic and celluloid images of World War II are so frequently used and reused that they have begun to supersede experience and memory. The power over such visual memory lies increasingly in the hands of those who create or manipulate such images. Indeed, producers of motion pictures and videos play a major role in the production and continuation of public memory of the war.

Around the 1970s, for example, a visual iconography of the Nazi era was projected in a number of acclaimed international art films. This was an imagery so powerful that it influenced subsequent motion pictures about the Third Reich. Luchino Visconti's *The Damned* (Italy–West Germany, 1969), Liliana Cavani's *The Night Porter* (Italy, 1974), Louis Malle's *Lacombe, Lucien* (France, 1974), and François Truffaut's *The Last Metro* (France, 1980) established conventions for the visual style of films about Nazism. But this imagery also meant that the Third Reich was often reduced to visual clichés: SS uniforms, swastikas, black leather boots and belts, imposing buildings, intimidating corridors, banners, and marble stairs. These became unmistakable emblems signaling Fascism, and they provided, unthinkingly perhaps, the entire historical background for the private personal episodes featured in these and later motion pictures.

Stereotypical images of the Third Reich evoked considerable controversy themselves. Some critics charged that they used fascist images mindlessly and that an inherent conservatism and sense of inevitability in such historical films depicted fascism as both fascinating and paralyzing.[24]

The Nazis themselves had emphasized the aesthetic perfection of mass: massed flags and more than 100,000 Germans in uniform, for example, filmed at giant rallies in Nuremberg. In such films, Nazi soldiers never march out of step. The regimentation inherent in National Socialism's propaganda was used against the Nazis by the Allied filmmakers in

World War II. Although there is truth in such images, their endless use as historical reality takes the place of and conceals all the unfilmed events and contributes to the homogenization of disparate individual experience.[25] Such powerful visual icons reinforce belief in uniformity and inevitability and restrict investigation of more complex and diverse experience actually present within the Third Reich.

In a 1974 interview about contemporary "Nazi-retro" films, French critic Michel Foucault argued that a battle had begun for the public memory of World War II. In this "battle for history, around history," as Foucault called it, he warned that whoever controls the collective memory of the people controls a nation's experience and the people's ability to act on the knowledge of the past.[26] He also criticized the filmic use of the Nazi era for erotic purposes.

More emphatically, Foucault denounced filmmakers' neglect of resistance movements that challenged the fascists in France and other European countries during World War II. There were no positive films about the resistance, he asserted, because conservative and even some liberal elements in postwar society wanted the resistance forgotten.[27] Instead, Foucault denounced what he saw as defeatist films that imply that no one was immune to fascism and thus nothing could be done about it. By manipulating the popular memory, erasing the recollection and remembrance of heroic resistance, and emphasizing instead the all-encompassing power of the Nazi occupiers, such fatalistic historical films, Foucault declared, emphasize popular apathy rather than empowerment, and thus played into the hands of the dominant powers in society.

Japan, as noted in the chapter by Freda Freiberg, has failed to come to grips with its wartime past, largely ignoring its military aggression and atrocities in World War II. Among the many examples of these, one has been the subject of a documentary: *In the Name of the Emperor* (U.S., 1995). It reminds viewers that Japanese soldiers raped and murdered tens of thousands of Chinese women at Nanjing in 1937 and 1938. Part of the film shows actual victims, being treated in hospitals, pictures taken at the time by the Reverend John Magee, an American missionary. That footage was available as evidence during the War Crimes Trials in Tokyo from 1946 to 1948.[28] Despite such undeniable evidence of these and other war crimes, Japan continues to face its wartime guilt reluctantly—if at all— evading the record of the past in a kind of national amnesia.[29]

A nation's unwillingness to face openly what happened in its past is not unique to our era. Instead, what concerns us here is that history (as presented in movie theaters and on television) supplements, and increasingly replaces, historical imagination and experience, and that filmmakers as yet have no agreed-on standards regarding the use and misuse of evidence and interpretation in such visual representations of the past.

Flouting the very idea of such standards, even producers of polemical historical films have found support from some film critics. Caryn James of the *New York Times* decries persons who "expect fact-based fictions . . . to be educational tools instead of art and entertainment." Dismissing "nit-picking about facts" as "narrow, pedagogical responses to movies [that] tend to be tremulous and fearful," James asserts that filmmakers need dramatic license to go beyond the facts. Indeed, they can present opinionated and even polemical interpretations in order to challenge established views of history, stimulate public debate, and (paraphrasing Faulkner) "discover the more profound truth of what might-have-been."[30]

The recent boom in historical films in the United States—such as Oliver Stone's *Nixon* (U.S., 1995) and his *JFK* (U.S., 1991), the latter the controversial director's depiction of President John F. Kennedy's assassination as the result of a conspiracy within the U.S. government to avoid withdrawal from the war in Vietnam—has contributed to the debate over the roles, the historical accuracy, and the acceptable degree of artistic license of such films.[31] It is not simply the factual errors in so-called petty details by some of those producing historical films that concern historians. More important is the lack of professional standards that allows the selective and distorted use of evidence to support what, under normally accepted rules of evidence, would be considered ridiculous conclusions.

For shock value or audience appeal or because they fit the ideological perspective of a particular director, the conclusions of such films can be impossibly extreme. *JFK* embraces a position rejected by every responsible professional historian of the subject.[32] Caryn James acknowledges that "there is a distinction between dramatic license and outright lying, of course. A film claiming that the Holocaust didn't happen, for example, would cross that line, going beyond dramatic license into sheer irresponsibility." Concluding that "the line itself can be fuzzy," James provides no answer for how to separate the big lie from the provocative statement or a thesis cynically adopted to provoke argument.[33]

The distinction, however, is crucial. The value of a historical film is that, through a skillful blending of images, words, and other sounds, it helps visualize the past and evoke a feeling for it. A historical film must necessarily compress events. But what differentiates allowable compression and restructuring of the past for dramatic effect or irresponsible and dangerous distortion?

While the majority of such films make reasonable and acceptable arguments—interpretations within the range of those accepted by historians and other serious students of the past—others violate every canon of evidence and argument. These are the films that not only adopt the most extreme interpretations, but support them with a consciously deceptive blending of fact and fiction. Distortion of the past is always problematic, but particularly so when dealing with the recent past. Fudging the facts in an American film about the life of Mozart or of Jefferson is of less immediate import than tendentiously misconstruing such recent events as the civil rights movement, the Kennedy assassination, or the Vietnam War—interpretations that continue to influence current society. The presentation as truth of Norman Mailer's "factoids"— "facts" that *may* be true—is a pernicious form of disinformation. As media critic Edward Jay Epstein, an authority on the Kennedy assassination, has stated concerning *JFK*, "When you mix fact with fiction you get fiction."[34]

In today's visually oriented world, powerful images—even images of images—are circulated in an eternal cycle, gaining increased acceptance through repetition. In Samuel Coleridge's classic fable, the Ancient Mariner obsessively reiterated his tale. Today's visual media frequently do the same. Thus history becomes an endless loop, in which repeated images validate and reconfirm one another. Globalized communications replicate identical memories in every region of our planet. Even as the past recedes, the electronic media instantly retrieve it and swiftly spread it over the entire world. As Anton Kaes suggests, today "history thus returns forever—as film."[35]

NOTES

1. Woodrow Wilson was shown *The Birth of a Nation* in the East Room of the White House on the evening of February 18, 1915, along with several other persons, including Thomas Dixon, author of the book on which it was based. Afterward, Wilson is alleged to have said, "It is like writing history with lightning. And my only regret is that it is all so terribly true." The president later denied that he had ever endorsed the controversial, highly racist film. Yet the remark has been widely accepted by historians, for example, John Hope Franklin, "*Birth of a Nation*—Propaganda as History," *Massachusetts Review* 20 (Autumn 1979): 425, 434; Michael Rogin, " 'The Sword Becomes a Flashing Vision': D. W. Griffith's *The Birth of a Nation*," *Representation* 9

(Winter 1985): 151; and Scott Simmon, *The Films of D. W. Griffith* (New York: Cambridge University Press, 1993), p. 112. However, Arthur S. Link, Wilson's preeminent biographer and the editor-in-chief of the most extensive edition of his papers, traced the quotation's first appearance in print to Milton MacKaye, "The Birth of a Nation," *Scribner's Magazine,* November 1937, p. 69, long after Wilson's death. Link noted that Dixon did not use the quotation in his memoirs, which have not been published, and that Marjorie Browning King, the only survivor in 1977 among the persons who had been at the White House screening, told him that year that Wilson had seemed lost in thought during the screening and had left the room afterward without saying a word (editorial note, in *The Papers of Woodrow Wilson,* ed. Arthur S. Link et al. [Princeton: Princeton University Press, 1980]), vol. 32, pp. 142, 267, 310–11, 455, 486–87).

2. Students of the philosophy of history continue to debate whether there is any "true" history that accurately and impartially reconstructs the "reality" of the past. Historians do agree, however, on accepted rules about the use of evidence.

3. D. W. Griffith, quoted in Kevin Brownlow, *The War, the West, and the Wilderness* (New York: Knopf, 1979), pp. 148–49.

4. This point is made in relationship to the classic films of World War I in Jay M. Winter, *The Experience of World War I* (New York: Oxford University Press, 1989), p. 328.

5. Samuel Hynes, "So Many Men, So Many Wars: 50 Years of Remembering World War II," *New York Times Book Review,* April 30, 1995, p. 16.

6. Anton Kaes, *From "Hitler" to "Heimat": The Return of History as Film* (Cambridge, Mass.: Harvard University Press, 1989), p. x.

7. Michael E. Geisler, "The Disposal of Memory: Fascism and the Holocaust on West German Television," in *Framing the Past: The Historiography of German Cinema and Television,* ed. Bruce A. Murray and Christopher J. Wickham (Carbondale: Southern Illinois University Press, 1992), p. 221.

8. For contemporary criticism of NBC's *Holocaust* series, see Elie Wiesel, "Trivializing the Holocaust: Semi-Fact and Semi-Fiction," *New York Times,* April 16, 1978, p. B1; Claude Lanzmann, "From the Holocaust to *Holocaust," Telos* 42 (Winter 1979–1980): 137–43; and Siegfried Zielinski, "History as Entertainment and Provocation: The TV Series 'Holocaust,' " *New German Critique* 19 (Winter 1980): 81–96.

9. The example of Warren Beatty's *Reds* also suggests that there may be subjects for which neither film and television nor historical monographs tell us what we want to know. John Reed's most important achievement was *Ten Days That Shook the World,* his account of the Bolshevik seizure of power in the fall of 1917. What allowed Reed, then in Russia, to collect documents quickly, have them translated, and then prepare an account of the Russian Revolution that was accurate in its outline as to what happened and its meaning? No written record of the book's gestation survives, only the finished product. Robert A. Rosenstone, in his fine biography of Reed, *Romantic Revolutionary: A Biography of John Reed* (New York: Knopf, 1975), can say little about how and why Reed's book was written.

10. Bruce Cumings, *War and Television* (New York: Verso, 1992), pp. 75–76. For Ken Burns's own view on the subject, see Thomas Cripps, "Historical Truth: An Interview with Ken Burns," *American Historical Review* 100, no. 3 (June 1995): 781–64. A

scholarly exchange on Burns's film is in Robert Brent Toplin, ed., *Ken Burns's "The Civil War": Historians Respond* (New York: Oxford University Press, 1996).

11. For changing responses to Jean Renoir's classic antiwar film *La Grande Illusion* (France, 1937), see Marc Ferro, "Film as an Agent, Product and Source of History," *Journal of Contemporary History* 18, no. 3 (July 1983): 363.

12. Robert A. Rosenstone, ed., *Revisioning History: Film and the Construction of a New Past* (Princeton: Princeton University Press, 1995), pp. 4–5 and passim. For a more traditional approach emphasizing the genre of the historical fiction film throughout the twentieth century, see Leger Grindon, *Shadows on the Past: Studies in the Historical Fiction Film* (Philadelphia: Temple University Press, 1994).

13. Kaes, *From "Hitler" to "Heimat,"* pp. 37–72, 105–60.

14. John Grierson, quoted in introduction to *Grierson on Documentary*, ed. Forsyth Hardy (New York: Praeger, 1971), p. 13. for a revisionist perspective on Grierson, see "John Grierson: A Critical Retrospective" [special issue], ed. I. C. Jarvie and Nicholas Pronay, *Historical Journal of Film, Radio and Television* 9, no. 3 (1989): 227–328.

15. Like the term "documentary," the word "propaganda" is often misconstrued. In fact, it is not always synonymous with falsehood, but rather connotes the shaping or controlling of information for specific purposes. In his study of the media and the Persian Gulf War, Philip Taylor argues that propaganda is a "process of persuasion" (*War and the Media: Propaganda and Persuasion in the Gulf War* [Manchester: Manchester University Press, 1992], p. 18).

16. Bill Nichols, *Representing Reality: Issues and Concepts in Documentary* (Bloomington: Indiana University Press, 1991), pp. ix–x.

17. A major discussion of the relationship between professional filmmakers and historians took place at the conference "Telling the Story: The Media, the Public, and American History," April 23–25, 1993, in Boston.

18. Interview with Jay Leyda, May 2, 1977, quoted in introduction to *Mission to Moscow* ed. David Culbert (Madison: University of Wisconsin Press, 1980), pp. 26–27.

19. Robert Abzug, *Inside the Vicious Heart: Americans and the Liberation of Nazi Concentration Camps* (New York: Oxford University Press, 1983).

20. At the time, Bruce Cumings had already written *The Origins of the Korean War,* 2 vols. (Princeton: Princeton University Press, 1987, 1990), and edited *Child of Conflict: The Korean–American Relationship, 1943–1953* (Seattle: University of Washington Press, 1983).

21. Cumings, *War and Television,* pp. 143, 3.

22. The consultants were Kevin Brownlow, David Culbert, and Martin Loiperdinger. For a good review of *Die Macht der Bilder,* see Hans-Joerg Rother, "Eine Prominente under den Unbelehrbaren," *Film und Fernsehen* 2 (1994): 50–52. See also the letter by Culbert and Loiperdinger printed in the *New York Times Book Review,* October 31, 1993, p. 55; and Loiperdinger and Culbert, "Leni Riefenstahl, the S. A., and the Nazi Party Rally Films, Nuremberg 1933–1934: *Sieg des Glaubens* and *Triumph des Willens,*" *Historical Journal of Film, Radio and Television* 8, no. 1 (1988): 3–38.

23. Kaes, *From "Hitler" to "Heimat,"* p. ix.

24. See the discussion in ibid., pp. 22–23, 218–19; and Robert Reimer and Carol Reimer, "Nazi-retro Filmography," *Journal of Popular Film and Television* 14, no. 2 (Summer 1986): 80–92.

25. For example, some rural communities in Germany were better able than urban areas to resist penetration by Nazi norms and controls, even during the war. See Jill R. Stephenson, "Triangle: Foreign Workers, German Civilians and the Nazi State: War and Society in Württemberg, 1939–1945," *German Studies Review* 15, no. 2 (1992): 339–59.

26. "Entretien avec Michel Foucault [Interview with Michel Foucault]," *Cahiers du cinéma* 251–252 (July–August 1974): 13, in which Foucault declared, "There is a battle for history, around history, that is taking place right now. . . . There is a desire to (en)code, to suppress, that which I call the 'popular memory [*memoire populaire*],' and also to propose to impose on people a filter of interpretation of the present."

27. Ibid., p. 8.

28. For films depicting Japanese war crimes, see Tzuping Shao, "John Magee's Documentary Footage of the Massacre in Nanjing, China, 1937–38"; Stephen MacKinnon, "Remembering the Nanjing Massacre: *In the Name of the Emperor* (1995)"; and Daniel J. Leab, "*In the Name of the Emperor:* War Guilt and the Medium of Film," *Historical Journal of Film, Radio and Television* 15, no. 3 (fall 1995): 425–38.

29. Nicholas D. Kristof, "Japan's Ruling Parties Divided over Push to Apologize for War," *New York Times*, June 4, 1995, p. A12. Confronted with direct evidence that the Imperial Japanese Army had conscripted Korean and other Asian women into prostitution for Japanese soldiers during the war, Tokyo offered an apology in 1993 but accepted neither legal nor financial responsibility for these victims. See Kazuko Watanabe, "Trafficking in Women's Bodies, Then and Now: The Issue of Military 'Comfort Women,' " *Peace and Change: A Journal of Peace Research* 20, no. 4 (October 1995): 501–15.

30. Caryn James, "They're Movies, Not Schoolbooks," *New York Times*, May 21, 1995, pp. H1, H18. James notes that in *Absalom, Absalom!*, one of William Faulkner's characters emphasizes the use of imagination to discover the truth about the past: "There is a might-have-been which is more true than truth." Although fiction can certainly provide insight into the past, this does not mean that all historical fiction is insightful or responsible. What is at issue is not the use of fiction to explain history or even to challenge currently dominant views of history. Rather, the question is whether irresponsible and dangerous historical fiction films should pose as nonfictional history.

31. The two largest professional historical associations in the United States, the American Historical Association (AHA) and the Organization of American Historians (OAH), have begun to debate such issues, including the relationship of professional historians to historical films and videos. See, for example, Harvey H. Jackson, "Can Movies Teach History?" *OAH Newsletter*, November 1990, pp. 4–5; William D. Jenkins, "Why TV Needs Historical Consultants," *OAH Newsletter*, November 1990, pp. 6, 23; and James Green, "Making *The Great Depression* for Public Television: Notes on a Collaboration with Documentary Filmmakers," *OAH Newsletter*, October 1994, pp. 3–6. A pioneering attempt to codify these difficult matters is contained in the AHA's Ad Hoc Committee on History and Film, "The Rights and Responsibilities of Historians in Regard to Historical Films and Video," *OAH Newsletter*, September 1992, pp. 15, 17.

On Oliver Stone's rewriting of history and grand conspiracy theory in *Nixon*, see the condemnation from different political perspectives in Stryker McGuire and David Ansen, "Stone Takes on Nixon," *Newsweek*, December 11, 1995, pp. 64–72; Richard Reeves, "Nixon Revisited by Way of the Creative Cinema," *New York Times*, December

17, 1995, pp. H1, 41; Maureen Dowd, "Nix 'Nixon'—Tricky Pix," *New York Times,* December 21, 1995, p. 14; and Jacob Cohen, "Nixon . . . Not," *National Review,* January 29, 1996, pp. 57–62.

32. Articles about Oliver Stone's *JFK* include "Twisted History," *Newsweek,* December 23, 1991, pp. 46–48; "When Artists Distort History," *Time,* December 23, 1991, p. 84; T. Bethell, "Conspiracy to End Conspiracies," *National Review,* December 16, 1991, pp. 48–50; "Oliver Stone's Paranoid Propaganda," *U.S. News & World Report,* January 13, 1992, p. 18; D. W. Berlin, "The Big 'Lies' of 'JFK,' " *New York,* February 17, 1992, pp. 44–47; and "Recapturing the Past," *Nation,* March 23, 1992, pp. 29–32. In *JFK,* Stone asserts the existence of a conspiracy within the U.S. government (FBI, CIA, Joint Chiefs of Staff, defense-industry representatives, and Vice President Lyndon Johnson) to kill the president in order to prevent U.S. military withdrawal from Vietnam. Although there is no historical consensus about the Kennedy assassination, *JFK* promotes an "interpretation" that has no support from professional historians. Does dramatic license allow producers to accept the most extreme theory? The producers of *Jefferson in Paris* (U.S., 1995) discovered that historians are unable to prove that Thomas Jefferson's alleged affair with one of his slaves did *not* happen; they used this absence of proof to claim that it *did* happen. Such "logic" suggests unlimited possibilities for rewriting history.

33. James, "They're Movies, Not Schoolbooks," p. H18; for some critical responses to James's article, see letters to the editor, *New York Times,* June 4, 1995, p. H4.

34. Edward Jay Epstein, quoted in Georgia Brown, "Patsies," *Village Voice,* March 31, 1992, p. 58.

35. Kaes, *From "Hitler" to "Heimat,"* p. 198.

Select Bibliography

Abrash, Barbara, and Janet Sternburg, eds. *Historians and Filmmakers: Toward Collaboration*. New York: Institute for Research in History, 1983.

"AHR Forum [on Portraying History on Film]." *American Historical Review* 93, no. 5 (December 1988): 1173–227.

Aldgate, Anthony, and Jeffrey Richards. *Britain Can Take It: The British Cinema in the Second World War*. 2nd ed. Edinburgh: Edinburgh University Press, 1994.

Allen, Robert C., and Douglas Gomery. *Film History: Theory and Practice*. New York: Knopf, 1985.

Anderson, Joseph, and Donald Richie. *The Japanese Film: Art and Industry*. Rev. ed. Princeton: Princeton University Press, 1982.

Avisar, Ilan. *Screening the Holocaust: Cinema Images of the Unimaginable*. Bloomington: Indiana University Press, 1988.

Baird, Jay W. *The Mythical World of Nazi War Propaganda, 1939–1945*. Minneapolis: University of Minnesota Press, 1974.

———. *To Die for Germany: Heroes in the Nazi Pantheon*. Bloomington: Indiana University Press, 1990.

Barkhausen, Hans. *Filmpropaganda für Deutschland im Ersten und Zweiten Weltkrieg*. Hildesheim: Olms, 1982.

Barnouw, Erik. *Documentary: A History of Non-Fiction Film*. 2d rev. ed. New York: Oxford University Press, 1992.

Basinger, Jeanine. *A Woman's View: How Hollywood Spoke to Women, 1930–1960*. New York: Knopf, 1993.

———. *The World War II Combat Film: Anatomy of a Genre*. New York: Columbia University Press, 1986.

Butler, Ivan. *The War Film*. South Brunswick, N.J.: Barnes, 1974.

Carnes, Mark C., ed. *Past Imperfect: History According to the Movies.* New York: Holt, 1995.

"Cinema, le temps de l'histoire" (Cinema, the Time of History) [special issue]. Ed. Christian Delage and Nicholas Roussellier. *Vingtième siècle: revue d'histoire* 46 (April–June 1995): 1–208.

Coultass, Clive. *Images for Battle: British Film and the Second World War, 1939–1945.* Newark: University of Delaware Press, 1989.

Cripps, Thomas. *Making Movies Black: The Hollywood Message Movie from World War II to the Civil Rights Era.* New York: Oxford University Press, 1993.

———. *Slow Fade to Black: The Negro in American Film, 1900–1942.* New York: Oxford University Press, 1977.

Culbert, David, ed. *Film and Propaganda in America: A Documentary History.* 5 vols. Westport, Conn.: Greenwood Press, 1990–1993.

Custen, George F. *Bio/Pics: How Hollywood Constructed Public History.* New Brunswick, N.J.: Rutgers University Press, 1992.

Davis, Natalie Zemon. " 'Any Resemblance to Persons Living or Dead': Film and the Challenge of Authenticity." *Yale Review* 76 (Summer 1987): 477–78.

Dick, Bernard F. *The Star-Spangled Screen: The American World War II Film.* Lexington: University Press of Kentucky, 1985.

Doherty, Thomas. *Projections of War: Hollywood, American Culture, and World War II.* New York: Columbia University Press, 1993.

Dolan, Edward F., Jr. *Hollywood Goes to War.* New York: Smith, 1985.

Doneson, Judith E. *The Holocaust in American Film.* Philadelphia: Jewish Publication Society, 1987.

Dower, John. *War Without Mercy: Race and Power in the Pacific War.* New York: Pantheon Books, 1986.

Drewniak, Boguslaw. *Der deutsche Film, 1938–1945: Ein Gesamtüberblick.* Düsseldorf: Droste, 1987.

Eiserman, Frederick A. *War on Film: Military History Education.* Historical Bibliography No. 6. Fort Leavenworth, Kans.: U.S. Army Combat Studies Institute, 1987.

Ferro, Marc. *Cinema and History.* Trans. Naomi Green. Detroit: Wayne State University Press, 1988.

Fielding, Raymond. *The American Newsreels, 1911–1967.* Norman: University of Oklahoma Press, 1972.

———. *The March of Time, 1935–1951.* New York: Oxford University Press, 1978.

Foucault, Michel. "Entretien avec Michel Foucault." *Cahiers du cinéma* 251–252 (July–August 1974): 5–18.

Furhammar, Leif, and Folke Isaksson. *Politics and Film.* New York: Praeger, 1971.

Fyne, Robert. *The Hollywood Propaganda of World War II.* Metuchen, N.J.: Scarecrow Press, 1994.

Garland, Brock. *War Movies: The Complete Viewers Guide.* New York: Facts on File, 1987.

Grenville, J. A. S. *Film as History: The Nature of Film Evidence.* Birmingham: University of Birmingham, 1971.

Grindon, Leger. *Shadows on the Past: Studies in the Historical Fiction Film.* Philadelphia: Temple University Press, 1994.

"Guerra, cinema i societat" (War, Film, and Society) [special issue], ed. J. M. Caparros-Lera, Sergi Alegre, and Luis Anyo. *Film Historia* 3, nos. 1, 2 (1993).

Gutman, Yisrael, and Michael Berenbaum, eds. *Anatomy of the Auschwitz Death Camp.* Bloomington: Indiana University Press, 1994.

Hay, James. *Popular Film Culture in Fascist Italy: The Passing of the Rex.* Bloomington: Indiana University Press, 1987.

"Historians and the Movies: The State of the Art" [special issue], *Journal of Contemporary History* 18, no. 3 (July 1983): 357–532.

"Historians and the Movies: The State of the Art" [special issue] *Journal of Contemporary History* 19, no. 1 (January 1994): 1–190.

Hoffmann, Hilmar. *"Und die Fahne führt uns in die Ewigkeit": Propaganda im NS Film.* Vol. 1. Frankfurt: Fischer Taschenbuch, 1988.

Hughes, Robert, ed. *Film: Films of Peace and War.* New York: Grove Press, 1962.

Hurd, Geoffrey. *National Fictions: World War II on Films and Television.* London: British Film Institute, 1984.

Insdorf, Annette. *Indelible Shadows: Film and the Holocaust.* New York: Random House, 1983.

Jarvie, Ian C. *Movies as Social Criticism: Aspects of Their Social Psychology.* Metuchen, N.J.: Scarecrow Press, 1978.

Jeancolas, J. P. *Quinze ans d'années trente: Le cinéma des français, 1929–1944.* Paris: Stock, 1983.

Jones, Dorothy B. "The Hollywood War Film: 1941–1944." *Hollywood Quarterly* 1 (1945): 1–19.

Jowett, Garth. *Film: The Democratic Art: A Social History of American Film.* Boston: Little, Brown, 1976.

Kaes, Anton. *From "Hitler" to "Heimat": The Return of History as Film.* Cambridge, Mass.: Harvard University Press, 1989.

———. "Holocaust and the End of History: Postmodern Historiography in Cinema." In *Probing the Limits of Representation: Nazism and the "Final Solution,"* ed. Saul Friedlander, pp. 206–22. Cambridge, Mass. Harvard University Press, 1992.

Kane, Kathryn. *Visions of War: Hollywood Combat Films of World War II.* Ann Arbor, Mich.: UMI Research Press, 1982.

Kenez, Peter. *Cinema and Soviet Society, 1917–1953.* New York: Cambridge University Press, 1992.

Koppes, Clayton R., and Gregory D. Black. *Hollywood Goes to War: How Politics, Profits and Propaganda Shaped World War II Movies.* New York: Free Press, 1987.

Kracauer, Siegfried. *From Caligari to Hitler: A Psychological History of the German Film.* Princeton: Princeton University Press, 1947.

Kyoto, Hirano. *Mr. Smith Goes to Tokyo: Japanese Cinema Under the American Occupation, 1945–1952.* Washington, D.C.: Smithsonian Institution Press, 1992.

Lawton, Anna, ed. *The Red Screen: Politics, Society, and Art in Soviet Cinema.* London: Routledge, 1992.

Leiser, Erwin. *Nazi Cinema.* Trans. Gertrud Mander and David Wilson. London: Seeker & Warburg, 1974.

Liehm, Mira. *Passion and Defiance: Films in Italy from 1942 to the Present.* Berkeley: University of California Press, 1984.

Loiperdinger, Martin. *Rituale der Mobilmachung: Der Parteitagsfilm "Triumph des Willens" von Leni Riefenstahl.* Opladen: Leske and Budrich, 1987.

Manvell, Roger. *Films and the Second World War.* South Brunswick, N.J.: Barnes, 1974.

Marwick, Arthur. *Class: Image and Reality in Britain, France, and the USA Since 1930.* New York: Oxford University Press, 1981.

Maslowski, Peter. *Armed with Cameras: The American Military Photographers of World War II.* New York: Free Press, 1993.

Mellen, Joan. *The Waves at Genji's Door: Japan Through Its Cinema.* New York: Pantheon Books, 1976.

Mintz, Steven, and Randy Roberts, eds. *Hollywood's America: United States History Through Its Films.* St. James, N.Y.: Brandywine Press, 1993.

Nichols, Bill. *Representing Reality: Issues and Concepts in Documentary.* Bloomington: Indiana University Press, 1991.

Nornes, Abe Mark, and Fukashima Yukio, eds. *The Japan/American Film Wars: Propaganda Films from World War II.* New York: Harwood, 1993.

O'Connor, John E. *Teaching History with Film and Television.* Washington, D.C.: American Historical Association, 1987.

———, ed. *Image as Artifact: The Historical Analysis of Film and Television.* Malabar, Fla.: Kreiger, 1990.

O'Connor, John E., and Martin A. Jackson, eds. *American History/American Film: Interpreting the Hollywood Image.* 2d ed. New York: Continuum, 1988.

Pronay, Nicholas, and D. W. Spring, eds. *Propaganda, Politics, and Film, 1918–1945.* London: Macmillan, 1982.

Raack, Richard C., "Historiography as Cinematography: A Prolegomenon to Film Work for Historians." *Journal of Contemporary History* 18, no. 3 (July 1983): 411–38.

Richards, Jeffrey, and Anthony Aldgate. *Best of British: Cinema and Society, 1930–1970.* London: Blackwell, 1983.

Richards, Jeffrey, and Dorothy Sheridan, eds. *Mass-Observation at the Movies.* London: Routledge, 1987.

Roeder, George H., Jr. *The Censored War: American Visual Experience During World War Two.* New Haven: Yale University Press, 1993.

Rollins, Peter, ed. *Hollywood as Historian: American Film in a Cultural Context.* Lexington: University Press of Kentucky, 1983.

Rosenstone, Robert A., "History in Images/History in Words: Reflections on the Possibility of Really Putting History onto Film." *American Historical Review* 93, no. 5 (December 1988): 1173–85.

——. "Revisioning History: Contemporary Filmmakers and the Construction of the Past: A Review Article." *Comparative Studies in Society and History* 32, no. 4 (October 1990): 822–37.

——. *Visions of the Past: The Challenge of Film to Our Idea of History.* Cambridge, Mass.: Harvard University Press, 1995.

——, ed. *Revisioning History: Film and the Construction of a New Past.* Princeton: Princeton University Press, 1995.

Sato, Tadao. *Currents in Japanese Cinema.* Toyko: Kodansha International; New York: Kodansha International/Harper & Row, 1982.

Shindler, Colin. *Hollywood Goes to War: Film and American Society, 1939–1952.* London: Routledge, 1979.

Short, K. R. M., ed. *Feature Films as History.* Lexington: University Press of Kentucky, 1981.

——, ed. *Film and Radio Propaganda in World War II.* Knoxville: University of Tennesee Press, 1983.

——, ed. *World War II Through American Newsreels, 1942–1945* [229 fiche]. Oxford: Oxford Microform, 1985.

Sklar, Robert. *Film: An International History of the Medium.* New York: Abrams, 1993.

——. *Movie-Made America: A Cultural History of American Movies.* Rev. ed. New York: Random House, 1994.

Sklar, Robert, and Charles Musser, eds. *Resisting Images: Essays on Cinema and History.* Philadelphia: Temple University Press, 1990.

Smith, Paul, ed. *The Historian and Film.* Cambridge: Cambridge University Press, 1976.

Sorlin, Pierre. *Esthétique d'audiovisuel.* Paris: Nathan, 1992.

——. *European Cinemas, European Societies, 1939–1990.* London: Routledge, 1991.

——. *The Film in History: Restaging the Past.* Totowa, N.J.: Barnes & Noble Books, 1980.

Staiger, Janet. *Interpreting Films: Studies in the Historical Reception of American Cinema.* Princeton: Princeton University Press, 1992.

Suid, Lawrence H. *Guts & Glory: Great American War Movies.* Reading, Mass.:
    Addison-Wesley, 1978.
Taylor, Philip M., ed. *Britain and the Cinema in the Second World War.* New York:
    St. Martin's Press, 1988.
Taylor, Richard. *Film Propaganda, Soviet Russia and Nazi Germany.* London:
    Croom Helm, 1979.
Taylor, Richard, and Derek Spring, eds. *Stalinism and Soviet Cinema.* New York:
    Routledge, 1992.
Thompson, Kristin, and David Bordwell. *Film History: An Introduction.* New York:
    McGraw-Hill, 1994.
Toplin, Robert Brent. "The Filmmaker as Historian." *American Historical Review*
    93, no. 5 (December 1988): 1210–27.
——, ed. *Ken Burns's "The Civil War": Historians Respond.* New York: Oxford
    University Press, 1996.
Virilio, Paul. *War and Cinema: The Logistics of Perception.* 2d ed. New York:
    Routledge, 1988.
Walkowitz, Daniel J. "Visual History: The Craft of the Historian-Filmmaker."
    Public Historian 7, no. 1 (Winter 1985): 53–64.
"War, Film, and History" [special issue]. *Historical Journal of Film, Radio and
    Television* 14, no. 4 (October 1994): 353–478.
Welch, David. *Propaganda and the German Cinema, 1933–1945.* New York:
    Oxford University Press, 1983.
——. *The Third Reich: Politics and Propaganda.* New York: Routledge, 1995.
Wetta, Frank J., and Stephen J. Curley, eds. *Celluloid Wars: A Guide to Film and the
    American Experience of War.* Westport, Conn.: Greenwood Press, 1992.
White, Hayden. "Historiography and Historiophoty." *American Historical Review*
    93, no. 5 (December 1988): 1193–99.
Williams, Linda. "Mirrors Without Memories—Truth, History, and the New Docu-
    mentary." *Film Quarterly* 46, no. 3 (Spring 1993): 9–21.
Winkler, Allan. *The Politics of Propaganda: The Office of War Information,
    1942–1945.* New Haven: Yale University Press, 1978.

Film and Video Sources

World War II has been memorialized in innumerable feature and documentary films, though it can sometimes be daunting to locate a particular one or to know where to obtain the best price for a particular title. Local video stores carry many classic World War II feature films and documentaries on videocassettes that can be rented or purchased.*

If the local video store proves insufficient, there are two large, expensive published guides to distributors of feature, documentary, and educational films and videos: *Bowker's Complete Video Directory*, 3 vols. (New Providence, N.J.: Reed Reference, 1995); and Anjanelle M. Klisz, ed., *Video Source Book*, 16th ed., 2 vols. (Detroit: Gale Research, 1995).

The following telephone and fax numbers of several distributors may also be helpful (numbers and prices were current as of November 1995 and are subject to change).

Direct Cinema
P.O. Box 10003
Santa Monica, Calif. 90410
(800) 525-0000; Fax (310) 396-3233

Videos of many films—including *The Life and Times of Rosie the Riveter* and *The Liberators*—for sale only.

A word of warning: many inexpensive video copies of films are incomplete or bowdlerized; inexpensive videos may also be of poor technical quality. Previewing is recommended before showing videos in the classroom. Naturally, the video format provides only a limited sense of the same film as projected in 35-mm film on a large screen in a motion-picture theater.

Facets Multimedia (or Facets Video)
1517 West Fullerton Avenue
Chicago, Ill. 60614
(800) 331-6197; Fax: (312) 929-5437

Videos for sale or rental. Facets Multimedia's catalog (for sale) lists thousands of titles, mostly features plus some documentaries from many countries. It is an important source for features from all over the world, including the former Soviet Union, and such films as *Ivan's Childhood* and *Come and See*, and sells video copies of *Men of Bronze*, *The Longest Day*, and the 1930 version of *All Quiet on the Western Front*.

International Historic Films
P.O. Box 29035
Chicago, Ill. 60629
(312) 927-2900; Fax: (312) 927-9211

Videos for sale only. International Historic Films is an important source for German feature films from the 1930s (many in German only) and Third Reich documentaries and newsreels as well as *Kolberg* (color, with English subtitles). It also carries a number of World War II documentaries and some titles relating to the Vietnam War. For European customers, videos are available in the two different formats used by European video systems: PAL (United Kingdom) and SECAM (France and Germany). NTSC is the video system used in the United States.

Motion Picture, Broadcasting, and Recorded Sound Division
Library of Congress
Washington, D.C. 20540
(202) 707-5709; Fax: (202) 707-2371

The division allows viewing only at the Library of Congress; films in the collection are neither sold nor rented. *Call at least two weeks in advance to reserve screening space.* Footage in the public domain may be copied, at commercial rates, for film productions. One of the most important film collections in the world, it is particularly strong in pre-1912 holdings and feature films. The collection has 16-mm print of *China Nights* and a video copy with English subtitles from the Japan Society, as well as a video copy of *Liberators*.

Movies Unlimited
6736 Castor Avenue
Philadelphia, Pa. 19149
(800) 668-3244; Fax: (215) 725-3683

Videos for sale only. Movies Unlimited Video Catalog (for sale) includes many foreign films either dubbed or with English subtitles. All videos are VHS/NTSC only.

Time Warner Viewer's Edge
P.O. Box 85098
Richmond, VA. 23285
(800) 544-1905; Fax: (203) 699-9586

Videos for sale only. Viewer's Edge offers a small free catalog and very low prices: for example, the 1979 color version of *All Quiet on the Western Front* costs $9.95; all seven of the Frank Capra *Why We Fight* films plus five additional wartime titles sell for $49.95.

Video Yesteryear
Box C
Sandy Hook, Conn. 06482
(800) 243-0987; Fax: (203) 797-0819

Videos for sale only. Video Yesteryear offers a free catalog that contains more than 1,000 titles. It is a good source for silent feature films, Holocaust documentaries, World War II American propaganda films, and American television programs from the 1950s and 1960s.

Contributors

Stephen E. Ambrose, military historian and biographer of Dwight Eisenhower and Richard Nixon; author of more than twenty books; professor of history and Director of the Eisenhower Center, University of New Orleans, Louisiana. Among his many books are *Crazy Horse and Custer*; *Rise to Globalism*; *Eisenhower*; *Nixon*; *Band of Brothers: E Company, 506th Regiment, 101st Airborne from Normandy to Hitler's Eagle's Nest*; *D-Day, June 6, 1944: The Climactic Battle of World War II*.

Erik Barnouw media historian, Emeritus Professor of Dramatic Arts at Columbia University and former chief of the Motion Picture, Broadcasting, and Recorded Sound Division at the Library of Congress. Producer of films, including *Hiroshima-Nagasaki, August 1945*. Author of numerous books, including the three-volume *History of Broadcasting in the United States*; *Documentary: A History of the Non-Fiction Film*; *Media Marathon: A Twentieth-Century Memoir*; *Tube of Plenty: The Evolution of American Television*; *The Sponsor: Notes on a Modern Potentate*; and *The Magician and the Cinema*.

John Whiteclay Chambers II, professor of history, Rutgers University, New Brunswick, New Jersey; Project Director, 1993–1995, Rutgers Center for Historical Analysis; scholarship on war, peace, and military institutions. Author of *To Raise an Army: The Draft Comes to Modern America*;

The Tyranny of Change: America in the Progressive Era; editor of *The Eagle and the Dove* and *The Oxford Companion to American Military History* (forthcoming); and co-editor of *The New Conscientious Objection: From Sacred to Secular Resistance*. He was a newswriter/producer at KRON-TV (NBC) in San Francisco, 1961–1965, and Director of Historical Research for *In Pursuit of Liberty* (U.S., 1977), a four-part public television series written and narrated by Charles Frankel at WNET (PBS) in New York City. He is completing a book on *All Quiet on the Western Front*, the antiwar film, and the image of World War I.

David Culbert, professor of history, Louisiana State University, Baton Rouge, Louisiana; scholarship on film in the World War II era, particularly in the United States and Germany; editor of the *Historical Journal of Film, Radio and Television*, the journal of the International Association for Media and History (IAMHIST); and author of *News for Everyman: Foreign Affairs in Thirties America*; *Mission to Moscow*; and the five-volume *Film and Propaganda in America: A Documentary History*. He was Director of Historical Research and Associate Producer for *Huey Long* (U.S., 1985), directed by Ken Burns. He is completing a book for Cambridge University Press entitled *Nazi Cinema Propaganda and the Riefenstahl Myth*.

Freda Freiberg, film historian and critic with a special interest in the issues of gender and ethnicity; lecturer on Asian cinemas at Monash University, Melbourne, Australia; scholarship on the Japanese film industry and Australian women's filmmaking. Author of *Women in Mizoguchi Films*; co-author of *Don't Shoot Darling! Women's Independent Filmmaking in Australia*; and co-editor of *Disorientations: Body/Gender/Culture*; as well as a regular contributor to Australian film journals.

Alice Kessler-Harris, professor of history and director of the Women's Studies Program at Rutgers University, New Brunswick, New Jersey; scholarship on women in the paid work force; author of *Out to Work: A History of Wage-Earning Women in the United States*; *A Woman's Wage: Historical Meanings and Social Consequences*; and *Women Have Always Worked*; and co-editor of *Perspectives on American Labor History: The Problem of Synthesis* and *U.S. History as Women's History: New Feminist Essays*.

Daniel J. Leab, professor of history, Seton Hall University, South Orange, New Jersey; editor of *Labor History*; scholarship on American film and labor history; publications include *Labor History Reader* and *From Sambo to Superspade: The Black Image in American Film*.

Peter Paret, Mellon Professor in the Humanities, School of Historical Studies, Institute for Advanced Study, Princeton, New Jersey; primary areas of research: European cultural history and the history of war. Among his many books are *Clausewitz and the State*, *The Berlin Secession*, *Art as History*, *Understanding War*, and *Persuasive Images* (with Beth Irwin Lewis and Paul Paret).

Clement Alexander Price, professor of history, Rutgers University, Newark, New Jersey; scholarship on Afro-Americans; author of *Freedom Not Far Distant: A Documentary History of Afro-Americans in New Jersey* and *Many Voices, Many Opportunities: Cultural Pluralism and American Arts Policy*.

Denise J. Youngblood, associate professor of history, University of Vermont, Burlington, Vermont; and a specialist in Russian popular culture and Soviet cinema; author of *Soviet Cinema in the Silent Era, 1918–1935* and *Movies for the Masses: Popular Cinema in Soviet Society in the 1920s*.

Acknowledgments

We thank those who made possible the conference "War, Film, and History" and consequently this book. A special acknowledgment goes to Peter Paret of the Institute for Advanced Study in Princeton, who provided invaluable advice and encouragement both personally and through his seminar on "Force in History" at the Institute (supported by grants from the Harry Frank Guggenheim Foundation and from J. Richardson Dilworth). The seminar, of which both the editors are members, takes a rewardingly broad view of its subject, ranging from mobilization of armed power to cultural reactions to war.

As the dedication of this book indicates, we are particularly indebted to the fellows and staff of the Rutgers Center for Historical Analysis (RCHA), where John Whiteclay Chambers was project director of the 1993–1995 project entitled "War, Peace, and Society in Historical Perspective." Rudolph M. Bell, then chair of the history department at Rutgers University, New Brunswick, and his successor, Ziva Galili, gave full support to the project. Lynn Shanko, RCHA associate director, provided unflagging assistance while carrying out all her other responsibilities at the center. Omer Bartov assisted with some translations. G. Kurt Piehler obtained some photographs from the National Archives. In addition, Michael Dobe and Barry Rusnock provided computer support. A number of student assistants at the RCHA helped us at various stages: Steven Adams, Ming Chan, Adam Jaffe, Hu Liang, Dina Moakley, Beth Griech Polelle, and Christy Snider. In Baton Rouge, James Hughes was particularly helpful.

Special thanks also to Laura Beard, Judy Blackman, and Jeff Hale in Baton Rouge for their computer expertise; Thomas J. Knock at Southern Methodist University, Dallas; Sam Gill at the Margaret Herrick Library of the Academy of Motion Picture Arts and Sciences, Los Angeles; Cooper Graham, Motion Picture, Broadcasting and Recorded Sound Section, Library of Congress, Washington, D.C.; Alison Pinsler in Los Angeles; Martin Loiperdinger of the Deutsches Institut für Filmkunde in Frankfurt; Hans and Gulla Dobrott and Hajo and Bärbel Grohmann in Berlin; and Tilman Westphalen, Thomas F. Schneider, Claudia Glunz, Dieter Voigt, Michael Fisher, Annegret Tietzeck, Nicole Figur, and other members of the faculty and staff of the Erich Maria Remarque Archive, Osnabrück, Germany.

We acknowledge particular intellectual gratitude, as well as our personal thanks, to Pierre Sorlin of the Université de la Sorbonne Nouvelle (Paris III) and Anton Kaes of the University of California, Berkeley.

In addition to those mentioned and to the authors of the essays in this book, we would like to thank other scholars at the conference "War, Film, and History" who provided such great insight into the subject: David Barnouw, Steven Brier, Catherine Clinton, Thomas Cripps, Bruce Cumings, Marion Deshmukh, Lloyd C. Gardner, Victoria de Grazia, Samuel Hynes, Susan Jeffords, Clayton R. Koppes, Jackson Lears, Vernon Lidtke, James M. McPherson, John E. O'Connor, Philip Taylor, Robert Brent Toplin, Alan Trachtenberg, Frank van Vree, Jay M. Winter, Virginia Yans, and Marilyn Blatt Young.

Financial assistance came from the Rutgers Center for Historical Analysis, the Research Council of Rutgers University, the Raoul Wallenberg New Jersey State Professorship in Human Rights, and the College of Arts and Sciences of Louisiana State University.

We would like to thank the International Association for Media and History and David Green, Publishing Director, and Carfax Publishing Company, publishers of the *Historical Journal of Film, Radio, and Television*. In addition, we would also like to thank the Deutsches Institut für Filmkunde and Gerhard Ullmann of the Filmmuseum, Munich. Thomas Rockwell gave us permission to publish the famous *Saturday Evening Post* cover of "Rosie the Riveter."

Finally, the editors wish to thank Nancy Lane, Irene Pavitt, and Helen Mules at Oxford University Press for so ably shepherding this book through to publication.

Index

Numbers in italics refer to pages on which illustrations appear.